CONSTRUCTIVE POSTMODERNISM

CONSTRUCTIVE POSTMODERNISM

Toward Renewal in Cultural and Literary Studies

Martin Schiralli

Ralph A. Smith and Matthew Kieran, *Advisory Editors*

BERGIN & GARVEY
Westport, Connecticut • London

Library of Congress Cataloging-in-Publication Data

Schiralli, Martin, 1947–
    Constructive postmodernism : toward renewal in cultural and
literary studies / Martin Schiralli.
        p.   cm.
    Includes bibliographical references and index.
    ISBN 0–89789–695–5 (alk. paper)
    1. Postmodernism.   2. Deconstruction.   3. Postmodernism
(Literature)   I. Title.
B831.2.S35   1999
149'.97—dc21   99–22081

British Library Cataloguing in Publication Data is available.

Library of Congress Catalog Card Number: 99–22081
ISBN: 0–89789–695–5

First published in 1999

Bergin & Garvey, 88 Post Road West, Westport, CT 06881
An imprint of Greenwood Publishing Group, Inc.
www.greenwood.com

Printed in the United States of America

The paper used in this book complies with the
Permanent Paper Standard issued by the National
Information Standards Organization (Z39.48–1984).

10 9 8 7 6 5 4 3 2 1

Contents

Introduction

To represent is to select, to select is to omit, to omit is to misrepresent.

A book could readily be written to show how the deconstructions of Jacques Derrida have energetically mined this conundrum[1] with notable success. The systematic representations of Rousseau, Saussure, Husserl, Lévi-Strauss, and many others whom Derrida has studied so intimately each *selects* certain ideas as its basic explanatory material. These grounding principles, functioning within each system as the source of what Derrida has called "presence" or "logos," are then theoretically driven to subdue or explain everything the selected ideas *omit*. One crucial thing they omit but which always resists subordination is the richly complex and often inexplicable play of meaning-in-writing itself. Though absent from explicit consideration within each system, this conceptual reality nevertheless wreaks silent havoc at its most important explanatory junctures. A deconstruction points to these stresses and inconsistencies within the language of the system itself and shows how these representational systems must effectively and invariably *misrepresent* that which they have sought to explain.

Well before the era of deconstruction, however, philosophers like Dewey and Wittgenstein approached their own versions of this conundrum in distinctive and productive ways. For Dewey, although no representation would ever, or could ever, be articulated in complete or infallible terms, ever more efficacious representations could be constructed if the concept of "thinking" were made to work in theoretical activities in the same integrated, naturalistic way thinking actually functioned in human experience. In a related fashion, Wittgenstein's later work painstakingly pursued efficacious representation in ever more richly observed and detailed, more "ordinary" and transparent, particular terms.

This book is about the different consequences each way of dealing with the conundrum of misrepresentation—the deconstructive and the constructive—has for our understanding of postmodernism and for cultural and literary studies.

Chapter One, "From Premodern to Postmodern," attempts to identify *one* source of the postmodern temperament in a reaction against twentieth-century modernism as the dominant cultural point of view from the turn of the century through the 1970s. Through examples taken from dance, visual art, photography, architecture, poetry, and philosophy, it is argued that postmodern preoccupations with ambivalence and indeterminacy represent a rejection of the modernists' reductive pursuit of "essential" sources of cognitive and aesthetic value. This aspect of modernism is, in turn, contextualized as a focused opposition to those forms of decorative, allusive, superficially idealized, and metaphysically expansive styles of art and thought that had reached a peak in the late 1890s.

Chapter Two, "The Lure of Derrida's Traces," identifies the principal underpinnings of the postmodern point of view respecting ambivalence and indeterminacy in the deconstructions of Jacques Derrida. In minutely examining Derrida's deconstructive program, this chapter uncovers a serious flaw in his crucial conception of *différance*, intentionally implying meanings deferred, which originates in his famous deconstruction of Saussure, from whose semantic principle, *différence*, Derrida's conception descends. Saussure's principle of differential meaning has well-acknowledged difficulties that are wholly independent of the problems identified in Derrida's deconstruction and that make *différence* ineffective as a semantic construct. That Saussure's general view must, at key junctures, effectively presume its opposite, as Derrida's deconstruction maintains, does not entail the conclusion that Derrida's *différance*, his supplement to *différence*, cures the prior theoretical difficulties in Saussure's semantic principle. Meanings deferred in *différance* presume prior meanings that Saussure's *différence* simply cannot produce. Chapter Two ends, therefore, with the possibility for productive meaning, meaning that is not perpetually deferred by the traces of other meanings that Derrida holds to be necessarily implicated in the operation of *différance*, still intact.

Chapter Three returns to postmodernism, but this time the focus is on another related source of influence: the philosophical rejection of the *modern*, that is Cartesian view of formal rationality and the related necessity of grounding philosophical systems in foundations of certainty. Although related to the "deconstructive postmodernism" already discussed, the relevant contributions of philosophers like Dewey, Wittgenstein, and Stephen Toulmin are presented as engaging uncertainty in productively meaningful ways. The term "constructive postmodernism" is proposed to refer to the general principles embedded in their orientations in order to startle us into an awareness that the epistemological difficulties uncovered by many deconstructive analyses are not new discoveries and that it remains possible to work productively and meaningfully within these limitations. "Constructive Postmodernism" is therefore the title of Chapter Three which concludes Part I of the book, "Postmodernisms."

Chapter Four, "Toward Renewal in Literary Studies," applies the principles of constructive postmodernism identified in Chapter Three to several areas of contemporary concern in literary studies. A notion of textual value, which may consist of aesthetic quality or cognitive quality or both, is proposed as a way of reorienting the study of texts on more flexible and comparative grounds. It reinforces the desirability of inquiring into the literary value of nonliterary texts as well as investigating the cognitive value of texts traditionally viewed as literary. The latter is particularly significant in terms of the postmodern preoccupation with the local and the particular, richly and thickly described, in contemporary social and behavioral science. As these sciences move increasingly into more descriptive, interpretive, and even figurative research strategies, textual scholars might wonder whether literary artists have anything special to offer in respect of furthering systematic understanding of social and behavioral phenomena.

Chapter Five, "Social Intelligence in Fiction," therefore, looks very carefully at novels by Jane Austen, Barbara Pym, and Anita Brookner in order to demonstrate that wholly apart from the aesthetic interest a novel may possess, a work like Jane Austen's *Mansfield Park* may also embody independently significant contributions to epistemology, semiotics, and methodological theory in the social and behavioral sciences.

Chapter Six, "Emotional Intelligence," continues the demonstrations of Chapter Five by mining the fictional accounts of E. M. Forster, Henry James, and Marcel Proust for empirically relevant contributions to contemporary work in psychology and philosophy on the emotions. With this chapter the second part of the book, "Toward Renewal," concludes.

NOTE

1. Although the problems embedded in the "conundrum of representation," are by no means original, their presentation here as a conundrum is the author's own device.

Part I

Postmodernisms

1

From Premodern to Postmodern

When the first ballerina rose on *pointe*, a defining moment occurred in the history of dance.[1] In bold and painful defiance of both gravity and physiology, the dancer's body was gracefully contorted as though a perfectly straight line ran from the hip and knee through the ankle and instep to the first toe. From this elevated point in time, new possibilities for elegant and beautiful movement would emerge in the choreography of both the French and Russian schools of ballet. The ascent of the ballerina's proportioned and disciplined body also provided new expressive possibilities, as the air itself came to supplement the ground as a creative medium for motion. The allure of the *pointe* was completed in the development of those special slippers of boxed white satin and ribbons, which, while offering little if any support to the foot, nevertheless permitted the imaginary line to be drawn perfectly in the viewer's mind right through the dancer's instep. The aesthetic triumph of graceful appearance embodied in the *pointe* conceals, however, a most unbecoming tyranny. If one were to visit the ballerina offstage just after a performance had concluded and observe the reality of those points of light and grace once their coverings have been undone, it could be quite revealing. Bruised and distorted by years of sustained abuse to the complex pedal musculature, a dancer's foot is often a painfully unattractive reality. Bones never designed to support such weight are enlarged and twisted in nature's best effort to cope with exigencies not anticipated in their evolutionary development, while the thickest calluses attempt to cushion a thousand unnatural shocks each day.

It will no doubt seem odd to seek out a key to the meaning of postmodernism in the iconology of a dancer's foot, but one is most assuredly there to be discovered. For just as postmodernism derives its ambivalent meanings from the rejection of modernism, so too does modernism derive its significance in opposition to *its* most immediate antecedents in thought and culture. Modern dance arises most emphatically in its rejection of premodern ballet by Isadora Duncan and Ruth St. Denis. "I am an enemy to the Ballet, which I consider a false and preposterous art,"[2] wrote Isadora Duncan in *My Life*. "Under the tricots are dancing deformed muscles . . . under the muscles are deformed bones."[3] Invited by Pavlova to observe her in a private class with the elderly master Petipa, who marked the time with a violin and "admonished her to greater efforts," Isadora Duncan sat for three hours:

> tense with bewilderment watching the amazing feats of Pavlova. She seemed to be made of steel and elastic. Her beautiful face took on the stern lines of a martyr. She never stopped for one moment. The whole tendency of this train-ing seems to be to separate . . . the movements of the body completely from the mind. The mind, on the contrary, can only suffer in aloofness from this rigorous muscular disci-pline.[4]

A visit very early the next day to the Imperial Ballet School revealed "all the little pupils standing in rows, and going through these tor-turing exercises. They stood on the tips of their toes for hours, like so many victims of a cruel and unnecessary Inquisition. The great, bare dancing-rooms . . . were like a torture chamber."[5]

As for Ruth St. Denis, when after only three days of lessons she balked at the contortions involved in achieving the third position of the feet, she departed the world of ballet for the liberation of the modern. If the premodern dance was unnatural and preposterous, the new, *modern* dance would be rationally reconstructed from more authentic first principles. Pared of the aberrant and artfully consoli-dated contrivances that disconnected the natural affinities between body and mind, what we would call today the kinesthetic sensibil-ity, modern dance could return to a more fundamental source of value. This source of value, the natural grace of free dramatic move-ment, would in turn hearken back to the deeply serious, even spiritual, role that dance had played in the ancient civilizations of Greece and Egypt. Here is the key to postmodernism that the modernist approach to dance provides. In its pursuit of the most genuine sources of kinesthetic value in the early years of this century, the revolution in dance begun by Duncan and St. Denis encapsulates a central feature of modernism which the postmodern attitude most centrally rejects: the view that it is not only possible to locate such fundamental sources of meaning and value, but that the artist or writer is obliged to pursue and tap these sources creatively and critically.

PROBLEMS IN DEFINING MODERNISM

Modernism, like postmodernism, is not a movement, though it is revealed in many movements in thought and culture. While futurists, imagists, vorticists, logical empiricists, and so on, did produce broadsides, tracts, and manifestos, these movements never actually organized themselves around explicitly stated core "principles" of modernism. Rather modernism, like postmodernism, is a concept that arises in cultural criticism in an effort to make sense of families of variously shared resemblances that run through a wide range of social and cultural achievements. The notion of family resemblances, here borrowed from Wittgenstein,[6] is a very helpful tool in understanding the nature and scope of both modernism and postmodernism. Often, as Wittgenstein demonstrates in his *Philosophical Investigations*, concepts in a living language are open-textured, accommodating complex purposes that defy our impulse to fix them in a defining set of necessary and sufficient conditions. Wittgenstein uses the example of "game" to illustrate the important point that no one essential feature is common to all legitimate instances of this term. Rather, all sorts of similarities in fairly complex patterns of relationship may be seen to link them, more loosely but still meaningfully, together.

Modernism, and ultimately postmodernism, is to be characterized, not defined, with respect to the sets of similarities and relationships that variously run through ranges of examples, much in the way that intergenerational family photographs display family resemblances. One can see similarities in the physical characteristics of groups of family members, different groups for different characteristics in crisscrossing networks of similarities, whose individual features variously appear here and there. While no one feature is common to all, some features in some families do seem more central than others. The most pervasive of such features in modernism, as exemplified in the origins of modern dance, is a drive to sweep away all irrelevant surface characteristics in all categories of cultural achievement, however sanctioned by tradition they might be, and to penetrate through to their simplest, most powerful essences. The finest achievements in art, literature, and philosophy, the modern attitude implied, would be thoroughly grounded in their respective first principles. This very significant feature of modernism may therefore be understood best in terms of an epistemologically reductionist temperament, a pursuit of the most foundational sources of cultural achievement. The modernist temperament also entailed an appropriately reductionist aesthetic. Use no "unnecessary" words, commanded the imagists to all poets, anticipating the modernist precept of Mies van der Rohe that "less" is more.

The most proximate motivations for the modern attitude were the historical accretions of conceits, conventions, decorations, routine allusions, and expansive metaphysical fantasies that had come to characterize late nineteenth-century culture and thought. The modernist attitude toward the old regime was impatient and disparaging. It was as if, T. E. Hulme[7] informed, a container of treacle had been spilled over the dinner table. The modernist imperative in all departments of thought and culture was wholly and briskly normative. Its key question for any category of cultural achievement was: What is the genuine source of value here? In modernist dance, as we have seen, the source of genuine kinesthetic value was not to be found in the apparent perfection of prescribed balletic positions and the tyranny of *la pointe*, but in the natural grace of dramatic movement in the modern dance of Duncan and St. Denis. For visual art, the sources of genuine visual value were not to be found in the idealized representations of harmonious proportions of a William Bouguereau but rather in the primacy of light among the impressionists and abstracted visual planes in the cubists. Nor was architectural value to be found in those eclectic premodern buildings whose various stylistic elements were manipulated to present the most fitting image for their owners, but rather in the primacy of function in determining form, as in the massively elegant glass towers of Mies.

THE POSTMODERNIST IMPERATIVE

Now, if there is a corresponding postmodernist imperative, it is to show that all such pursuits of genuine value are fundamentally misguided. Wary of all talk of grounding value or even meaning and knowledge in essential foundations, the postmodern attitude regards human meanings as too fragile and indeterminate to support any such inquiry. While the postmodern creative imperative is to illustrate these fragilities and ambivalences, indeed, to tease and play with them disruptively and even sometimes dangerously, the postmodern critical imperative is to challenge the very conceptual frameworks within which in can appear to make sense to ask such a question as "What is the genuine source of value here?"—let alone answer it successfully. The justifications for this view will be examined minutely in the next chapter, for it is the deconstructions of Jacques Derrida that attempt to show, through his notion of *différance*, how systems that try to ground meaning or knowledge or value in first principles inevitably fail because an endemic ambivalence or undecidability always infects their attempts.

But enough has just been said to permit bringing the discussion of dance already begun to its postmodern conclusion. If one takes the work of Merce Cunningham as a model of the postmodern approach to dance, a work like the 1966 *How to Pass, Kick, Fall, and Run* may be seen to contain important features of what we have come to call postmodernism. Here the purposeful merger of movement and music is displaced by a soundscape of anecdotes randomly and ironically recited by the aleatory composer John Cage. The union of mind and motion prized by the modern dance advocate is severed in the randomness of the disciplined dissociation of the dancers' movements from any particular stimuli. The inherent momentum of movements themselves as they randomly occur propels the intentionally derailed choreography of *How to Pass, Kick, Fall, and Run.* Cunningham's dancers respond to purely physical sensations rather than artfully matching specific, meaningful movements to particular expressive intentions. Here movement, sound, language and meanings collide, instigate, or are displaced in an ongoing process of indeterminacy. In the work of other postmodern dancer-choreographers like the contemporary Kazuo Ohno, plainly deconstructive dimensions of cultural displacement and ambivalent gender add further features to the range of characteristics that distinguish postmodern dance.

Similarly, postmodern visual art and architecture reject the pursuit of grounding principles altogether and deliberately and perversely play with visual ambiguity and expressive ambivalence. Postmodern buildings are once again alive to eclectic inspiration, often ironically allusive, and to decoration, while the contemporary postmodern sculpture of a Duane Hanson at once displaces both the premodern preoccupation with idealized representation and the modernist absorption in visual essences by minutely recreating effigies of ordinary people in mundane situations with a deadly accurate eye. This postmodern trend is also present in photography where neither the sensuously romanticized premodern qualities of Julia Margaret Cameron's nineteenth-century portraits nor the modernist revelations of interior personal qualities produced in the portraiture of Edward Weston survive the deadpan, frontal assault of German photographer Thomas Ruff's unmediated masterpieces of postmodern portrait study.

In the burgeoning field of postmodern cultural studies, the same sort of discontinuity may be observed between theorists like Jean-François Lyotard and Jean Baudrillard and their modernist predecessors. If the reductive cultural analyses of Freud in *Civilization and Its Discontents* represents repudiation of the morally elevated, eclectic critical plane of premodern cultural analysts like Ruskin and Arnold, then the deconstructive analysis of theoretical "metanarratives" in Lyotard's *The Postmodern Condition* may likewise be seen to repudiate a whole set of reductive critical perspectives.[8] Whereas Freud exhibited a modern preoccupation with explaining culture in terms of vestigial and nonsocial visceral impulses mediated by an ego itself under the stressful influence of socially achieved codes of behavior and propriety, Lyotard's famous postmodern incredulity extends even to that other engine of modern cultural criticism, Marxism, in which the modern condition was to be explained, also reductively, in terms of economic variables like surplus value. For Lyotard the postmodern work on incredulity and metanarratives represented an abandonment of his own prior Marxist orientation. In seeking out the far side of such incredulity, Jean Baudrillard also repudiates the cramped determinism of a Marxism with which he too previously was enamored. In so doing Baudrillard actively chooses to pursue instead a new and dizzying pursuit of the "sublime" based not, like its original formulations in the eighteenth and nineteenth centuries, on an awareness of natural *immensity* but rather on awareness of the ultimately unrepresentable *complexity* of human experience.[9]

MODERNIST POETRY

Abhorrence of clutter and a desire to identify basics are characteristics of modernism that are also very significant in the development of poetry. For the modernist poet, value was not to be found in the rituals of metronomic conformity and elevated, decorated diction that had come to characterize the premodern Georgian poets, but rather to be sought in the perceptually precise diction of the musically significant but formally naturalistic *vers libre* of Ezra Pound and T. S. Eliot. Pound had settled in London, just prior to the First World War, as the chief advocate of a radically new poetic. Urging an immediate break with the substance and style of most English-language poetry then being written, Pound quickly became the chief codifier, explainer, and proselytizer for the new approach to verse. The sense of high purpose that focuses Pound's formative contributions to modernist poetics is apparent in his formally published essays like "How to Read" and with even greater urgency in his correspondence. Pound's early letters document a passionately committed advocacy directed to publishers, writers, poets great and small, and even to *les jeunes*, like the young Iris Barry, aspiring to write better verse. The letters to Iris Barry[10] are particularly significant in that over an extended correspondence Pound quickly assumed the role of friend, mentor, and teacher, giving excellent advice on what to read and how to write. If these letters provide an *ad hoc* textbook of the new poetics, then in a letter to the publisher of *Poetry*, Harriet Monroe in 1915, Pound provides a *précis* of the curriculum.[11] Here Pound counsels strongly against all forms of indirect or unnatural usage in poetic diction and urges more concrete, undecorated language in pursuit of genuine poetic power. Poetic diction must contain nothing that one could not actually say. Stripped of the rhetorical clutter that had come to suffocate premodern verse, *vers libre* literally represented a form of stylistic liberation for the modernist poet, in the same way that the modern developments in dance that Duncan and St. Denis were promoting so intently sought to secure for their art.

In "How to Read," Pound set out the modernist position on the genuine sources of poetic value quite plainly:

> If we chuck out the classifications which apply to the outer shape of the work, or to its occasion, and if we look at what actually happens in, let us say, poetry, we will find that the language is charged or energized in various manners.
>
> That is to say, there are three "kinds of poetry":
>
> • Melopoeia, wherein the words are charged, over and above their plain meaning, with some musical property, which directs the bearing or trend of that meaning.
> • Phanopoeia, which is a casting of images upon the visual imagination.
> • Logopoeia, "the dance of the intellect among words," that is to say, it employs words not only for their direct meaning, but it takes count in a special way of habits of usage, of the context we *expect* to find with the word, its usual concomitants, of its known acceptances, and of ironical play.[12]

If T. S. Eliot's "The Love Song of J. Alfred Prufrock" may be taken as an exemplar of poetic modernism, then its opening evocation of a London evening will be seen to exploit fully all of Pound's categories of poetic meaning. Here the unsettling images of etherized patients and tawdry hotels that are presented to the visual imagination work strategically against the softly reassuring cadences of the verse, creating literally insidious semantic tensions that impel the reader toward the "overwhelming" question ultimately and ironically to be revealed. Inasmuch as the disjointed verbal context imparts energy to the poem, as does the perverse vividness of the imagery and the sound directing, not following, the sense, all three elements of the modernist poetic may there be seen perfectly illustrated.

MODERNIST METAPHYSICS

In looking to philosophy, another characteristic of the family of modern resemblances moves more centrally into focus, for in philosophy the "modern" as distinct from the "modernist" reaches much further back in time, indeed, to the origins of modern philosophy in the seventeenth century. Like their more recent modernist relations, modern philosophers were preoccupied with foundations; but unlike their medieval or ancient ancestors, they were additionally committed to a model of rationality that was essentially mathematical in its structure and dynamics. In a later chapter this aspect of the modern will be developed at some length, but for the present it should suffice to note that the modernist philosopher is also, importantly, a modern philosopher. Modernist philosophers at Cambridge University like Russell, Moore, and Wittgenstein (in his first philosophical career) sought first principles not in the mannered idealism of F. H. Bradley's undifferentiated Absolute, but in a pristine, clear, and perfectly rationalized form of logical empiricism. It has become a commonplace of the history of English-language philosophy in this century to point to the "revolt" of Bertrand Russell and G. E. Moore at Cambridge early in the twentieth century as the beginning of philosophical analysis, for until their work commenced in earnest, British philosophy was firmly in the thrall of a very pure form of metaphysics. Unlike the subtle, covert or implicit forms of presence that Derrida is so adept at exposing, the work of Bradley and McTaggart, the immediate predecessors of Russell and Moore, had devoted careers to the unapologetic production of vast metaphysical systems built with great complexity and dexterity upon the grounding presence of idealism. There are, of course, important methodological antecedents in the English-language empiricist tradition prior to the rise of nineteenth-century British idealism; the eighteenth-century Scottish philosophers of common sense, Reid and Stewart, share much in the way of linguistic orientation and methodology with Moore and Russell and to a surprising and insufficiently noted degree also with Wittgenstein and J. L. Austin. In terms of their most recent philosophical colleagues, however, Moore and Russell certainly did effect a fundamental reorientation to more traditional British preoccupations with logic and language. Understanding the nature of the relationship between language and the world that Russell's reorientation produced and the implicit presence of structure that Wittgenstein was to develop and delimit so forcefully in his *Tractatus Logico-Philosophicus* will ultimately be of enormous help in providing links from the *différance* of Derrida to the notion of productive meaning.

Spurred by his successes with Whitehead in expressing mathematics in the language of formal logic, itself an exemplary modernist project, Russell saw the possibility of applying the same methodology to an analytic reconstruction of the language of scientific theories. Russell intended to integrate philosophy and science in order to provide the methodological infrastructure needed to develop an accurate picture of the world and a grounded understanding of the real limits of knowledge. Implicit in the program begun in his "Logical Analysis"[13] paper were a set of metaphysical assumptions regarding the nature of language and its relationship to the world; these assumptions involve the essence and, therefore, the possibilities of language rather than the contingent vagueness and mistakes that happen to be embedded in language as it is ordinarily used. In this linguistic essence Russell and the later positivists saw the real possibility of creating an ideal language to be used in gathering and developing empirical knowledge through science, ably assisted by the new philosophy. For Russell the essential structure of language was directly anchored in the essential structure of the world, a form of logocentric presence very similar to that implicit in Saussure and, more obviously so, to that in mature structuralist theory. Russell's world was comprised of "things" and "facts." Following Leibniz, Russell maintained that it was intuitively obvious that any complex entity must be comprised of simples, and to these simples he applied the term "things." Things exist in relation to other things and their own properties such that any relationship between a thing and its own properties or another thing is a "fact"—in the case of the simples described here, an "atomic fact." In principle, then, determining the truth or falsity of a proposition would involve comparing what the proposition purports to tell us with the fact described in the proposition. The truth of the proposition turns on the accuracy of the correspondence between itself and the fact. Propositions that are themselves complex need analysis (often with the ready assistance of the new philosophers) into simple propositions such that all complex or "molecular" propositions may be seen to be verifiably reducible to atomic propositions.

Atomic facts all share the same formal structure, "this that," which captures the "things in relations" notion just sketched. The choice of "this" and "that" suggests the means by which language was to be anchored to the world: ostension. Those properties, for example, that like colors were for Russell simples were attached to reality by ostensive definition. Pronouncing "red" while pointing to something red sufficed, for Russell, in fixing the meaning of "red." Unlike red, however, most of the concepts of ordinary discourse were vague and muddled, with what we say and how we say it obfuscating the actual nature of things. For scientific knowledge to be truly firm, a logically purified, "ideal" language would have to be achieved that could provide the means of naming through ostension the newly isolated simples that constitute the world. The epistemological ramifications of this view were stark and modernistic: what we could know with certainty about the world was the truth and falsity of simple and formally analyzable complex propositions. Except for tautologies, propositions that neither admitted of verification as atomic facts nor were in principle reducible through logical analysis to such atomic facts were simply a species of nonsense.

These basic ideas were to be given elegant expression and sophisticated refinement in Wittgenstein's *Tractatus Logico-Philosophicus*, which Wittgenstein believed represented upon its completion nothing less than the solution, at least in essentials, of all genuine problems in philosophy. So thoroughly did Wittgenstein believe in his achievement that upon the completion of the *Tractatus* he left Cambridge and philosophy, ultimately to begin a new career teaching primary school in rural Austria. During his absence from philosophy, Wittgenstein's *Tractatus* became through the admiring efforts of Russell and the Vienna Circle positivists the central theoretical foundation of logical empiricism. What attracted these positivists most in Wittgenstein's work was what Wittgenstein himself valued least in his book: the demonstration of what could be said meaningfully in language. Significant empirical propositions were not nearly so important to Wittgenstein as that which was, according to the *Tractatus*, beyond the reach of literal language. If he had solved all the problems of philosophy, "then the value of this work secondly consists in the fact that it shows how little has been done when these problems have been solved."[14] He had solved the problems of philosophy only so as to identify the important problems of life, those ethical and spiritual dimensions that resist propositional representation. "Whereof one cannot speak," Wittgenstein concludes, "thereof one must be silent."[15]

The "world" of the *Tractatus* was philosophically an advance on Russell's world in at least two important ways. Where Russell had only vague, implicit metaphysical presuppositions, Wittgenstein delimited fully and plainly the nature of the validating basis for the logical empiricist view. To move from the noumenal substance, that which exists independently of what is the case, to the analysis of complex propositions, Wittgenstein develops a concise and unnervingly comprehensive metaphysical system in which the concepts of "facts," "states of affairs," "negative facts," "thoughts," "propositions," and "sense" are interdependently elaborated with clarity and rigor. The second advance is of great importance for the present inquiry since it has to do with the theory of meaning that Wittgenstein develops to account for the possibility of language truly representing the world. It is Wittgenstein's own deconstruction of this theory in his later work that creates the possibility for a theory of productive meaning that does not rest upon the kind of validating presence at work in the *Tractatus* and in the deconstructions of Derrida previously mentioned.

Wittgenstein's theory of meaning in the *Tractatus* is a "picture" theory of meaning in which we picture facts to ourselves. Like those of Russell, these facts are constitutive of the world; they are objects or simples in relations. In picturing facts our mental pictures share the same "logico-pictorial form" with the fact so pictured, the picture thus "reaches right out"[16] to reality. It is this isomorphism of form, this structural correspondence, that anchors language to the world. Through the presence of logico-pictorial form, a pictured fact is a thought; a thought, a proposition with a sense. Hence, linguistic meaning is thoroughly grounded in the world. Wittgenstein, of course, like Russell, is not making claims here about the actualities of language, but about the possibilities inherent in the essence of language. With this admission, however, the doctrine runs into grave difficulties, difficulties that the positivists ignored, but that Wittgenstein himself acknowledged. If, as the general Russell-Wittgenstein view proclaims, the only things, apart from tautologies, that can be significantly said are propositions that either purport to describe a fact or can by means of analysis be reduced truth-functionally to such elementary propositions, surely the propositions in Russell's "Logical Atomism" and Wittgenstein's *Tractatus* must, insofar as they fit into no category of significant proposition, be senseless. This fundamental incoherence in logical positivism, so like the basic logocentric contradictions identified in Derrida's deconstructions, lay silently waiting to be properly understood.

Most significant, Wittgenstein did not ignore this incoherence within the text of the *Tractatus* itself; hence the famous disclaimer near the end of the work:

My propositions serve as elucidations in the following way: anyone who understands me eventually recognizes

them as nonsensical, when he has used them—as steps—
to climb up beyond them. (He must, so to speak, throw
away the ladder after he has climbed up it.) He must tran-
scend these propositions, and then he will see the world
aright.[17]

Unlike the philosophically inconvenient demonstrations of inconsistency in Derrida's deconstructions, for Wittgenstein this anomaly
is an unembarrassing consequence of his early view. Apprehending
the nature of the world and language, like every other important
insight, can only be shown, not said.[18] The picture theory of meaning that the *Tractatus* develops is, in the last analysis, a work of modern art whose value lies in an elegantly developed heuristic trope.

Wittgenstein took his responsibilities teaching school children in
Austria very seriously, carefully developing strategies for initiating
them into wider and more various conceptual territories. In the actual processes of teaching his students new concepts, he grew much
less confident that the "picture" of meaning rendered in the *Tractatus*
was sound. His level of dissatisfaction with his earlier solutions led
eventually to his return to Cambridge and to a reconsideration of
the problems of philosophy. Many of the demonstrations in his *Philosophical Investigations* are actually an assault on his own earlier work,
relentlessly deconstructing the theory of meaning embedded therein.

The opening sections of the *Investigations* are directed precisely at
the foundations of this theory of meaning. "A *picture* held us captive," writes Wittgenstein. "And we could not get outside it, for it
lay in our language and language seemed to repeat it to us inexorably."[19] It is the picture of a neat *Verbindung* or isomorphism between
language and the world. Words attach meaningfully to objects in
relations because there is a one-to-one correspondence between the
logical possibilities inherent in the structure of thought and language
and the structure of the world and its component simples. Linkages
among these isomorphic structures are effected in the actualities of
language use and acquisition through the principle of ostension.
Pointing to any object in the world while saying the word used to
refer to it would suffice to establish an ostensive definition of the
word and form a meaningful link to the mental picture that internally represents it. One sees here a powerfully attractive picture,
one that fits comfortably with many intuitive understandings and
that presents the possibility of true descriptions of states of affairs,

of a true composite description of reality in which the general form of a proposition describes plainly how things are. But now Wittgenstein acknowledges that although one "thinks that one is tracing the outline of the thing's nature over and over again . . . one is merely tracing round the frame through which we look at it."[20]

In a very important way the *Philosophical Investigations* represents Wittgenstein's own deconstruction of his earlier modernist views. It is perhaps ironic that this most powerful deconstruction is fashioned by the same philosopher who produced, in his earlier work, the most successful articulation of modernist metaphysics and epistemology. Before returning to Wittgenstein, however, it essential to discuss the postmodern philosophical contributions of Jacques Derrida to the business of deconstruction and to give fuller significance to his key notions of *différance* and *archi-écriture*.

NOTES

1. Dancing *sur la pointe* was first introduced into ballet around 1830, at the time of Taglioni. For more details see Gail Grant's *Technical Manual and Dictionary of Classical Ballet*, 2nd ed. (New York: Dover, 1967).

2. Isadora Duncan, *My Life* (New York: Horace Liveright, 1927), p. 164.

3. Fredrika Blair, *Isadora: Portrait of the Artist as a Woman* (New York: McGraw-Hill, 1986), p. 29.

4. Duncan, *My Life*, p. 165.

5. Ibid., p. 166.

6. See Ludwig Wittgenstein, *Philosophical Investigations*, 3rd ed., trans. G.E.M. Anscombe (New York: Macmillan, 1968), p. 31.

7. See T. E. Hulme, "Romanticism and Classicism," in *Prose Keys to Modern Poetry*, ed. Karl Shapiro (Evanston, Ill.: Harper & Row, 1962), pp. 91–104.

8. For more on Jean-François Lyotard, see his *The Postmodern Condition: A Report on Knowledge*, trans. Geoff Bennington and Brian Massumi (Minneapolis: University of Minnesota Press, 1993).

9. Jean Baudrillard's special form of the sublime may be pursued in *Simulacra and Simulation*, trans. Sheila Faria Glaser (Ann Arbor: University of Michigan Press, 1994), and his *Selected Writings*, ed. Mark Poster (Stanford, Calif.: Stanford University Press, 1988).

10. See Ezra Pound, *Selected Letters*, ed. R. D. Paige (New York: New Directions, 1968), pp. 76–91.

11. Ibid., p. 49.

12. Ezra Pound, "How to Read," in *Literary Essays*, ed. T. S. Eliot (New York: New Directions, 1968), p. 25.

13. Bertrand Russell, "Logical Atomism," in *Logical Positivism*, ed. A. J.

Ayer (New York: Free Press, 1959), pp. 31–50.

14. Ludwig Wittgenstein, *Tractatus Logico-Philosophicus*, trans. C. K. Ogden and F. P. Ramsey (London: Kegan Paul, Trench, Trubner & Co., 1922), p. 29.

15. Ibid., p. 189.

16. Ludwig Wittgenstein, *Tractatus Logico-Philosophicus*, trans. D. F. Pears and B. F. McGuinness (London: Routledge & Kegan Paul, 1961), p. 9.

17. Ibid., p. 74.

18. See Allan Janik and Stephen Toulmin, *Wittgenstein's Vienna* (New York: Simon and Schuster, 1973) for an excellent, detailed treatment of Wittgenstein and the logical positivists. It is particularly important for challenging the stock notion that Wittgenstein was a positivist himself.

19. Wittgenstein, *Investigations*, p. 48.

20. Ibid.

2

The Lure of Derrida's Traces

It sees the world as contingent, ungrounded, diverse, un-
stable, indeterminate, a set of disunited cultures or interpretations which breed a degree of skepticism about the
objectivity of truth, history and norms, the givenness of
natures and the coherence of identities.

—Terry Eagleton
The Illusions of Postmodernism

Terry Eagleton here is writing on the style of thought that has come
to characterize much of the humanities in the era of postmodernism
and deconstruction.[1] For those scholars who still view literary texts
as exemplars of cultural significance and value, his characterization
will have much resonance, as the era of deconstruction has indeed
produced a number of unsettling developments. In the hands of
postmodern practitioners, for instance, the activities of literary criticism seem no longer concerned to elucidate or contextualize the aesthetic or social achievements of important writers, but rather these
newer critiques attempt to show that texts are incapable of bearing
any stable meaning, durable reference, or distinctive value whatso-
ever. Once prized as creative artifacts whose multilayered significance tapped fundamental regions of personal and cultural meaning, literary texts are now often viewed merely as objects embody-

ing pernicious internal contradictions and the metaphysical (and other) misapprehensions of their authors.

To deconstruct a text, effectively, is to show how it is internally subversive of its own devices: that the rhetorical stance it assumes is a conceit, a construction built on illusory foundations; and regardless of what the author intends to express, or is taken by sympathetic readers to express, texts will inevitably be betrayed by their own language into revealing the underlying mistakes and confusions manipulating the consciousness of writers and their more conventional readers. Since texts have no meaning or reference except in interpretation and as interpretations are idiosyncratic, or even delusory, there can be no tenable basis for adjudicating among alternative readings. Hence a literary scholar's pursuit of meaning and significant value in literature is a foolish quest. The task of the truly deconstructed critic is rather to expose texts, to display their surface tensions, and to reveal their covert commitments.

The following pages attempt first to argue and then to demonstrate by extended illustrations that, notwithstanding the formidable challenges to literary criticism presented by deconstruction, it remains possible and desirable to speak productively about literature and to continue to seek novel ways in which literary texts may be seen to enhance our experience and our understanding. Although the illustrative chapters that follow are deliberately wide in scope, the argument that follows in this chapter will be limited to a careful reading of Jacques Derrida, the inventor of deconstruction, for it is Derrida's original formulations that lie at the center of deconstructive criticism and from which its most interesting applications descend. Perhaps no other writer in the twentieth century has had so profound an influence on the humanities as this wholly original, chimerical genius; much of postmodernist culture is in one way or another linked in fundamental ways to his startling insights. The brilliance of his exegetical *tours de force* must be acknowledged even by those critics who believe him to be wrong; and if his methods are antic and inverted, his purposes are nonetheless serious and philosophical. It is not surprising, however, that the intellectual integrity of Derrida's thinking is often questioned by his critics, as in the spectacular controversy surrounding the honorary degree he received from the University of Cambridge in 1992. Approaching Derrida often breeds frustration and anger since even the most patient reader can easily become disoriented and confused in his perversely purposeful divagations. To have read Derrida is to know what it means to watch a squirrel dance on an invisible rope.

Because Derrida occupies such a central place in deconstruction and postmodernism, very close attention to critical components of his views can yield far-reaching dividends. If it can be shown in what follows that Derrida, in the development of his thinking and at a fundamental choice point in discovering a serious problem in Saussure's conception of linguistic *différence*, takes a turn to epistemological indeterminacy that is both intrinsically incoherent *and* unnecessary, then it may be seen to be reasonable to reject the subsequent, provisional findings and methods that he and his followers promote. Such an argument here cannot aim simply to reject these findings, however, because it is an essential part of Derrida's thinking to present these investigations as unrestricted explorations of the play of language-in-writing, the very nature of which perpetually defers closure and conceptual clarity. Moreover it must be quickly admitted that what follows below is a rational reconstruction of that part of Derrida's thinking that touches on issues of semantics. As a reconstruction, it *must* be seen by anyone who has accepted Derrida's provisional program as an intrinsically misleading account. On the other hand, there is no alternative available to one who is ultimately not persuaded by Derrida and who has not forsaken the potential efficacy of rational disputation. Other than a silent rejection or an angry fulmination, *attempting* to engage Derrida in argumentative terms would seem the only productive strategy. Although it cannot allay these concerns, it is also important to note that every effort has been made in the reconstructive process to produce for this formidable writer a "strong" rather than "straw" man position. What Derrida *has* provided in place of systematic theory is an intimation of newer ways of thinking about language and human consciousness powerfully illustrated in a series of close readings, or deconstructions, of a group of texts that have provoked his thinking. Some of the most important of these deconstructions comprise the bulk of Derrida's most influential book, *Of Grammatology*, a text of central importance to contemporary literary scholarship.

Notwithstanding the provisional nature of Derrida's investigations, these explications have produced one core insight: that the pursuit of grounding an epistemology in an ultimately validating metaphysical principle is a self-defeating process. Derrida's undeniable contribution to the history of thought lies in demonstrating through painstakingly minute analyses that Rousseau, Nietzsche, Husserl, and Heidegger are each undermined by internal inconsistency on this point and that the structuralist views of Saussure and Lévi-Strauss, even as they seek to establish systemic, relational loci of meaning, likewise succumb to a very similar ailment. It is very important, however, in considering Derrida on these writers to keep the following question in mind, especially since Derrida declines on principle to offer a positive account of his own views: Even if one concurs in Derrida's diagnoses of these thinkers, is one obliged to accept his view that the process of grounding meaning in metaphysical principles is always unproductive? Or would one more modestly conclude that the thinkers Derrida has analyzed had simply not succeeded in their tasks and leave the larger question open for further consideration?

A variant of this question will also usefully be borne in mind: Even if Derrida is right about the impossibility of grounding meaning in metaphysical principles, that is, that logocentric theories of meaning are internally self-defeating, are *all* attempts to ground meaning likewise self-defeating? Or may we identify persuasive sources of rational stability in many of our meanings and in the judgments that support them?

As Derrida's thinking develops interactively in criticism of his chosen authors, in the following discussion the two principal approaches to meaning that preoccupy Derrida's deconstructive analyses are first presented in some detail. The characterizations of the structuralist account of meaning in Saussure and Lévi-Strauss and the phenomenological account of meaning in Husserl are intended as brief but sympathetic representations of these views. Derrida's deconstructions of these positions aim at revealing internal inconsistencies: that in creating theories that depend upon fundamentally privileged binary oppositions of presence and nonpresence, these writers succumb to the inevitable derailment that accompanies all attempts to fix meaning in unproblematic first principles. It will take a bit of exposition and analysis to present Derrida's key notion of *différance* properly and to give adequate intelligibility to the previous sentence, but for the moment simply noting that for Derrida this notion, and the semantic instabilities it entails, both enlivens and *threatens* human experience will help explain why we seek, again and again, to ground meaning in some durable basis. We create theories of meaning and reality, Derrida's deconstructions imply, because we are uneasy with the indeterminacy inherent in human consciousness. Subliminally sensing danger in this ambivalence, we therefore attempt to stabilize thinking by representing reality in manageable terms. For Derrida, the persistent conceptual tools in this process are binary opposition and "presence."

Such binary systems begin with what is taken to be a solid and unshakable foundational principle. This core concept, the source of all the system's explanatory power, is regarded by the formulator and followers of the system as manifestly true and capable, with the patient and careful construction of supportive theory, of making sense of everything its binary opposite entails. This core concept in Husserl's phenomenology is interior intuition, specifically the privileged perspective on reality that intuitive bracketing provides in our efforts to penetrate to the true nature of things. In the structuralism of Saussure and Lévi-Strauss, it is the primacy of the direct apprehension of structural concepts that provides the foundation of the system's explanatory framework. In both the structuralist and phenomenological cases, one binary term is presumed to be safely grounded and beyond dispute. This term provides a baseline of security against the dangers of conceptual instability that we dread. Derrida calls this term variously the *logos* (following the ancient Greek tradition) or the source of *presence* (following Heidegger) or simply the first term in a comprehensive binary system of thought.

As our propensity to formulate binary structures is based on our need to pursue a measure of control over the instabilities inherent in our intellectual experience, developing such grounded systems has been the continuing aim of traditional philosophy. All philosophical systems are, therefore, ostensibly validated in an unproblematic presence or logos. Logocentrism for Derrida is merely a way of naming the explicit or implicit presumption that it is possible and meaningful to ground meaning and knowledge in such a validating principle. Logocentrism may be observed most explicitly in metaphysics, the branch of philosophy that systematically pursues first principles; but the (often implicit) metaphysical grounding of meaning and knowledge in some form of presence, Derrida would maintain, is at the foundation of all systematic thought, even those positions whose proponents would resist vehemently any suggestion that they were at all metaphysical. In short, all systematic accounts of meaning and knowledge are built upon foundational binaries in which the first, the privileged, term or logos is used to subordinate or subdue any concerns associated with the second, opposite term.

With these key elements of Derrida's thinking in place, a deconstruction may now be more clearly described as an attempt to undermine the possibility of logos itself in that it displaces the binary principle of a system by an exegetical process that purposefully disrupts the whole system. The deconstructive analyses of Saussure and Husserl discussed hereafter involve reversing the terms of the foundational binaries, treating the second term as privileged and subordinating the first. In this way each system's implicit conceptual stratagems are made explicit, and the resulting deconstructions show how the relevant texts must be undermined by the very epistemological ambivalence they are seeking to subdue. This endemic undecidability or indeterminacy always "infects" such theories, and while the virus may never be cured, a deconstruction will at least make the affecting condition plain. It is tempting, almost compulsively so, for Derrida to ferret out these inevitable ambivalences at critical junctures, because he believes, as the discussion of his reading of Saussure provided later will show, that epistemological ambivalence permeates all thought. Although denied or ignored in traditional thinking, this ambivalence is unavoidably, creatively, disruptively, dangerously at work in all human thought and language. Indeed, in the thinking of Derrida himself, the ambivalence of *différance* is actively embraced in pursuit of conceptually counter-intuitive forms of originality.

Phonocentrism is that form of presence in which speech is the privileged binary term and writing is its intrinsically weaker derivative. It has deep roots in the Western tradition: From Plato through Rousseau, Saussure, and Lévi-Strauss, the primacy of speech over writing has been a common presumption. In deconstructing their accounts, Derrida shows that writing may successfully function as the privileged term, with speech in the subordinate position; and that even though these writers are committed logically to the priority of speech, they must inevitably at times write in a way that presumes its opposite to be so. Intrinsic ambivalence leads inexorably to self-contradiction.

Derrida's approach to meaning, the focus of this chapter, is thoroughly enmeshed in his deconstructions of Saussure and Lévi-Strauss. His reading of Saussure is particularly significant in that it provokes Derrida's fullest development of the key notion of "trace." The following attempt to explicate the development of this pervasive element in Derrida's thinking will lead directly to the sources of his most problematic and contentious notions: *différance* and *archi-écriture*.

SAUSSURE

In Ferdinand de Saussure's revolutionary *Course in General Linguistics*, the "sign" is the union of concept and sound image. The concept is the "signified"; the sound image or word is the "signifier." While it would seem eminently plausible to keep such fundamental theoretical concepts distinct, it is important to note that Saussure chooses to present them as different aspects of the same unified sign. Unlike all prior systematic study of language, which treated the history of specific words as a key to their contemporary meaning, in Saussure's account the relationship between signifier and signified is arbitrary, that is, the actual phonemic symbol for "book" is in no way necessary to the concept of "book." Other sounds serve to mark out the concept just as well in other languages. Moreover, just which features of what we see as a book *that will be essential to the concept of book* are not simply established in the activity of naming. That "book" involves covers, for instance, may only be discovered by examining how the signifier is situated in an entire system of signifiers, and this situation is a feature of language as a socially achieved whole.

Meaning for Saussure, therefore, arises diacritically (differentially or relationally) from the signifier's relationship with all other signifiers within the language-as-system, through the principle of *différence*. We recognize different occurrences of the word book, for example, not because it may be defined in terms of inherent qualities but because it is situated in a system, defined as an element in the structural whole of language. Book is distinguished semantically from "cook," "took," "shook," and so on, by the roles that the initial phonemic differentials concerned play in the system of language. This language-as-system or code is called *langue*, in Saussure's theory, while ordinary speech events or utterances are designated as *parole*. The proper study of linguistics is the synchronic study of the "code" governing speech events rather than the diachronic study of the history of specific speech events. The scientific study of language is the study of the system, code, or *langue*.

At this point a feature of Saussure's theory, first identified as a paradox by Roland Barthes, must be noted. In this theory meaning arises within *langue* but *langue* is derived from *parole*. The semantic linkages embedded in Saussure's notion of the unified "sign" are silently transported from *langue* to *parole* without theoretically engaging the paradoxical bridge at all. In this way meaning can appear to be a purely systemic phenomenon, because the differential elements that produce linguistic meanings are derived from differences among signs *as* sound images. But as sound images are "merged" in the unified sign with *meaningful concepts*, Saussure is poised, semantically, *to appear* to have it both ways: "Everything that has been said up to this point boils down to this: in language there are only differences. Even more important: a difference generally implies positive terms between which the difference is set up; but in language there are only differences *without positive terms*."[2]

This is much more than a minor problem because the union between sign and signified represents whatever semantic energy the theory can have. If meaning is established and validated in the actual uses of language (*parole*) by groups of people with distinctive purposes in an ongoing process of developing representational possibilities, then it is only in *parole* that the sign is actually meaningfully connected to the world. If this is so, then meaning cannot be wholly explained in systemic terms (*langue*). Saussure's sign, therefore, must implicitly presume linkages among language, thought, and the world, in order for *différence* to have any semantic force. This in turn will be a problem for Derrida because, even though he has other important criticisms to make of Saussure's *différence*, he is silent on this one. Indeed, it is the nonpositive, systemic view of meaning inherent in *différence* that Derrida seeks to develop further in his own concept of *différance*.

The requisite theoretical attempt missing in Saussure is adumbrated by Lévi-Strauss[3] in the process of formulating a comprehensive theory of structuralism. In mature structuralist thought, language becomes a general structuring faculty, with Saussure's differential possibilities anticipated in and recognized through "structures" inherent in the mind itself. Although these general structures of mind, exemplified in the connectedness of *langue* and *parole* in the structured human mind, become a kind of neo-Kantian (or commonsense Kantian, as Lévi-Strauss prefers) validating presence in the classic formulations of structuralism, they are *not* embedded in Saussure's purely systemic notion of *différence*.

As already intimated, it will be shown later that this huge anomaly in Saussure's theory is an equally compelling problem for Derrida and deconstruction; linking the two problems is the concept of *différence*, so central to the development of Derrida's thinking. Indeed a more satisfactory perspective on meaning as a variable convergence of agreements of judgments among language users must be deferred until the discussion of Wittgenstein resumes in the next chapter. For the present it will suffice to emphasize here that in Saussure's account words are held to function meaningfully through the principle of *différence*, or the patterns of diacritical relationships that situate them within the structure of *langue*. For Saussure, therefore (and very problematically), the fixed patterns of *différence* can produce definite inventories of meaning.

ARCHI-ÉCRITURE AND *DIFFÉRENCE*

It is another anomaly in Saussure's conception of *différence* that provokes Derrida's supremely counter-intuitive view that writing must be logically prior to speech. That anomaly will be much more readily formulated if it is approached indirectly, from the perspective of "grammatology" and the view of writing embedded in it. Grammatology, in Derrida's formulation, is the approach to the study of language that treats writing, in a general, pretextual sense, as the origin of all language, including speech. By having this pretextual writing or *archi-écriture* subsume speech from the outset and in claiming that this view of language is latently prefigured in Saussure, Derrida appears quite adroitly well-defended against a binary deconstruction of his own view. Derrida finds the necessary linkages between *différence* and *archi-écriture* implicitly established in Saussure even as his predecessor explicitly seeks to dismiss writing as a variously incomplete graphic representation of speech.

In order to make these linkages plain, Derrida's grammatological deconstruction of Saussure disrupts the privileged position of speech or *parole* in the theory (in which writing is "explained" in terms of speech) by showing how writing (now functioning disruptively as the privileged term in which speech is to be understood) is unavoidably at work in Saussure's discourse. Derrida's deconstruction attempts to show that not only must Saussure resort to using writing as a source of illustrative examples for paradigmatically nongraphic linguistic phenomena, but that even when Saussure

> is not expressly dealing with writing, when he feels he has closed the parentheses on that subject, that Saussure opens the field of a general grammatology. Which would

no longer be excluded from general linguistics, but would dominate it and contain it within itself. Then one realizes that what was chased off limits, the wandering outcast of linguistics, has indeed never ceased to haunt language as its primary and most immediate possibility. Then something which was never spoken and which is nothing other than writing itself as the origin of language writes itself within Saussure's discourse. Then we glimpse the germ of a profound but indirect explanation.[4]

This "something" may be observed in the paradoxical nature of the relationship between *langue* and *parole*:

Saussure says of language: "Language is necessary for speech to be intelligible and to produce all its effects; but speech is necessary for language to be established; historically, the fact of speech always comes first." There is a circle here, for if one rigorously distinguishes language and speech, code and message, schema and usage, etc., and if one wishes to do justice to the two postulates thus enunciated, one does not know where to begin, nor how something can begin in general, be it language or speech. Therefore, one has to admit, before any dissociation of language and speech, code and message, etc. (and everything that goes along with such a dissociation), a systematic production of differences, the *production* of a system of differences—a *différance*—within whose effects one eventually, by abstraction and according to determined motivations, will be able to demarcate a linguistics of language and a linguistics of speech, etc.[5]

Here is the anomaly in Saussure's *différence* discovered by Derrida. *Différence* can only work if it presumes a system out of which differences may be purposefully abstracted. *Différence* presumes a differential framework, a *différance*, Derrida claims as he pointedly displaces an "e" with an "a," that moves freely among differential possibilities in a system of what will ultimately be described as perpetual deferral.

Importantly for Derrida, *différence* needed to be articulated just as Saussure had intended for this potent ambivalence to be discovered. It is for this reason that Derrida has said that Saussure's structuralism was a necessary stage in the development of grammatology and deconstruction. Writing, the medium of *différance*, which itself "is the origin of language" and which is implicitly at work in Saussure, is far more authentic than falsely grounded speech. If speech cannot truly be grounded in a validating presence, then writing, or *archi-écriture*, is uncontaminated by mistakenly relied-upon delusional forms of presence and logos. Writing, after all, is by its very nature language in its uncorrupted, unpresent, state and in its general, nontextual form, *archi-écriture*, must be logically prior to its misrepresentation in logocentric theories of speech. As immune to the false comfort of presence and therefore free of the corrupting constraints of an impossible and obscuring metaphysics, this pretextual writing permits the free pursuit of the full range of the possibilities of meaning. With writing thus identified as simply the free play of meaning possibilities, meaning itself may be seen to reside in the free play of Derrida's *différance*.

There is an enormous difference between *différence* and *différance*, for it is upon the latter notion of *différance*, which Derrida offers as the inevitable supplement to Saussure's, that the entire deconstruction of Saussure turns. If, in Saussure's system, a given differential element conveys meaning, it can only *function* as a differential element *within the context of its relevant set of differential elements*. The operation of *différence* that produces a meaning in Saussure's system actually requires the implicit participation of a host of other differential elements, each of which, on Saussure's own account, is sufficient to produce yet other meanings. Derrida justly observes that *différence* cannot yield definite meanings at all, but rather sets in play an *in*-definite array of meaning possibilities, in which "an element functions and signifies, takes on or conveys meaning, only by referring to another past or future element in an economy of traces."[6]

All of Saussure's differential elements are invisibly present as "traces" whenever any one element of the set comes into play. Within this economy of traces, meanings are pulled and stretched along crisscrossing networks of association and displacement in a perpetual process of deferral. In just such a way the concept of the trace itself stretches and displaces Saussure's determinate *différence* and transforms it into Derrida's indeterminate *différance*, in which the idea of deferral is the critical element. As all relevant traces are always implicated in any specific meaning, all specific meanings must ultimately be indeterminate. And as all purposefully abstracted "differences," like that between a linguistics of speech and a linguistics of language (mentioned earlier) must rely upon this ambivalent system of meaning possibilities—this economy of traces—as its differential medium, theoretical closure on any issue is perpetually forestalled.

Derrida often uses derailment metaphors in connection with pursuing the insidious lure of the trace. Unpacking these metaphors, it is as if all our activities of thinking and meaning proceed like a train whose tracks are continually merging with new branch-lines of track, whose multiple junctions are governed by switches that are often beyond our control. Some branches lead to further branches, some to inert sidings, and still others simply run out of track. Those branches that lead into new and richly subbranched lines of track follow the trace creatively and productively into great writing (literature, genuine theory, original thinking), while those branches that run out of track and derail the train follow the trace dangerously to potential catastrophe. Thus is Saussure's theory "haunted" by the traces of *différance*, by a primal writing or *archi-écriture* that flows directly from Derrida's explication of the unintended, unwanted consequences immanent in, and ultimately deconstructive of, Saussure's notion of *différence* itself.

This fuller articulation of the idea of the trace now permits a succinct reconstruction of Derrida's view of writing as *archi-écriture*: Writing may be considered as the free play of the trace in thought and language, with this free play of the trace functioning in Derrida's thinking as a locus of human consciousness. This locus of human consciousness is writing or *archi-écriture* and is freer than speech in that it does not depend upon a mistakenly privileged linkage between the signified and the signifier. The price to be paid for this freedom, however, is the abandonment of the false hope and delusional security of grounded, determinate meanings. All of the most aberrant features of deconstruction may now be properly understood. If the locus of human consciousness is writing or *archi-écriture*, then the Derrida's most famous (or infamous) epigram, "*Il n'y a pas de hors-text*,"[7] becomes transparent and lucid, for there can be nothing outside of the text. All deconstructions must be ultimately inconclusive since they are by their very nature perversely defiant of the myths of logos and presence. Distinctions between literature and philosophy are tiresome and untenable since both are at the mercy of the play of the trace and either may equally lead to insight or to dead ends.

HUSSERL

Another principal spur to Derrida's reliance on *archi-écriture* and the trace is a set of deconstructive readings in phenomenology that immediately precede those in structuralism. This set of explications aims to deconstruct another theory that grounds meaning in presence, although in the case of Edmund Husserl, Derrida is dismantling his earliest philosophical commitments as well. In the first edition of *Logical Investigations* (1901), Husserl distinguished between the Kantian noumenal and phenomenal worlds, restricting phenomenology to the study of the thing as it is given to us and not to the thing as it is itself. But in *Ideas Pertaining to a Pure Phenomenology and Phenomenological Philosophy* (1913), Husserl claimed that the noumenal thing in itself can be known intuitively as the identity given, in noematic analysis (or the phenomenological description of the object), to us in a variety of appearances. Husserl maintains that through noetic analysis (the phenomenological description of subjective intentions) the nature of perception, memory, and the like may be intuitively known. In these forms of phenomenological analysis, we use a process of free variation or imaginative analysis aimed at teasing out the essential features of the object or intention under consideration. In both cases we look for some y (or feature) without which some x (an object or intention) would lose its identity. If imagining x without y destroys x, then y is an essential feature of x. This process, eidetic intuition, reveals the eidos or essence of an x, and in this way eidetic intuition reveals necessary or apodictic truths about objects or intentions. Meaning therefore is phenomenologically reduced to an internal condition of consciousness in that it is independent of any contingent externals like actual sounds or symbols. This presence of the internal involves a structural isomorphism between reality and the mind.

Derrida insists that the only way to make such a view of meaning plausible is (silently) to presume the (implicit) participation of the externals (the conventional differentials of Saussure, for example) in the eidetic process, thus defeating the internal/external binary upon which Husserl's theory of meaning rests. Thus deconstructed, Husserl's failed attempt only reinforced Derrida's interest in the problems of structuralism and his developing reliance on traces and *différance* in analyzing meaning in fundamentally ambivalent terms.

DIFFÉRANCE AND INDETERMINACY

But is this reliance justified? Does the internal inconsistency revealed in Derrida's deconstruction of Saussure automatically entail the plausibility of traces and *différance*? The connective tissue in this development in Derrida's thinking is of enormous importance and well worth careful analysis. It is precisely in Derrida's move from *différence* to *différance* that the indeterminacy of meaning so crucial to deconstructive thinking and all that it has influenced finds its animating semantic principle. Understanding this move is therefore critical not only in any attempt to come to terms with Derrida's view of meaning, but also because the view of ambivalent meaning that *différance* entails undergirds so much of the postmodern fascination with relativism in literature, history, law, and social science. Consequently very much depends upon whether and to what extent Derrida's move to *différance* from *différence* makes sense and upon just what kind of sense it might make.

Since *différance* is a supplement to *différence*, the semantic adequacy of Saussure's account of meaning is of central importance. But, as noted in the discussion of Barthes's paradox, there is a large problem here for Derrida. While no one disputes the enormous contribution Saussure made to modern linguistics, even so sympathetic a critic as Jonathan Culler has noted:

> One might argue that Saussure's distinction between the purely formal and differential value of the signified in the linguistic system and its positive signification in actual use has hampered the development of an adequate semantics of language. Attempts to describe the signified in terms of relational features, which have worked so well for the phonemes of the signifier, have proven singularly unsuccessful; and it may well be that semantics would have progressed more rapidly if Saussure had not asserted the priority of value over signification. It seems likely that an adequate semantics will have to take the speech act as its basis and restore, at least to some extent, the ancient rights of *parole*. But one can scarcely reproach Saussure for his failure in this domain, since he at least recognizes the im-

portance of semantics more clearly than did his immediate successors, and since no one, even in recent years, has solved the fundamental problems of semantics.[8]

If we assume, only for the moment, that Culler is right and that Saussure's theory of meaning is not a very strong or persuasive one in that the *différence* that works "so well for the phonemes of the signifier" has "proven singularly unsuccessful" in producing an adequate semantics or theory of meaning, then what precisely has Derrida shown in his deconstruction of Saussure?

The concept of the trace, which arises in its semantic aspect from Derrida's critique of Saussure's differential elements, proceeds on the presumption that *différence* can in fact produce meanings. Derrida's deconstruction shows only that *within the conception of meaning encompassed by Saussure's account* those meanings will not be univalent or determinate due to the implicit presence of the entire relevant set of meaning-producing differential elements, as traces, in any specific instance of meaning. If Saussure's conception of meaning is inadequate, as the analysis of the "merged" sign given earlier suggests and as Culler claims the history of semantics shows, then the semantic inadequacies in Saussure inevitably infect Derrida's supplement as well, displacing *différance* from its position as an account of deferred meaning. If *différence* in Saussure is semantically vacuous, then Derrida's traces entail not indeterminate meanings at all, but nonmeanings. Unless one can show that Saussure has (or can be made to have) a productive and plausible semantics, Derrida's *différance* is not a coherent view of meaning at all. The play of the trace might be seen to reconstruct, brilliantly, the complex patterns of confluence among the streams of human consciousness, but the meanings within the streams, for all that Derrida has written, could still be determinable.

That Saussure's theory of differential meaning can only proceed by presuming its opposite, as shown by Derrida's deconstructive analysis of *différence* and traces, therefore in no way entails the conclusion that Derrida's notion of *différance*, however provisional or tentative he may claim it to be, eliminates the prior semantic vacuity in Saussure's concept. Meaning deferred presumes prior meaning. Absent Saussure's covertly validating sign, whence comes such meaning? If *différence* cannot adequately account for meaning in the first place, then Derrida's demonstration of its internal inconsistency only reinforces the inadequacy of that view; it does not move us inexorably to the free play of the trace as the only alternative, or indeed as the most plausible alternative way of thinking about meaning.

There is a more fundamental difficulty for Derrida in Saussure's theory, however, than that of internal inconsistency, for one could argue that if Saussure's account is "repaired" to provide some of the required bridges so that it might be more theoretically efficacious in respect of meaning, then it might save Derrida's *différance* as well. Even if one were to provide theory to connect *différence* more plausibly than Saussure has done to the semantic possibilities of the sign, as later structuralists attempted, the notion of *différance*, however, would still be implicated in Saussure's implicit phonocentrism, which Derrida must reject. The complexity of this issue is further compounded by the fact that Derrida is probably right about the impossibility of grounding meaning in the structural presence of speech, but for reasons different from the ones he offers. Derrida's *différance*, therefore, needs Saussure's *différence* to be capable, at least in principle, of accounting for meaning in order for his supplement to derail the possibility of determinate meaning. Absent that capability, the deconstruction shows only that Saussure's theory is unsuccessful.

SAUSSURE AND CONTEMPORARY SEMANTIC THEORY

Saussure's contribution to our understanding of language and semiology is so immense and his insights so prescient and compelling, that it must be emphasized that whatever failure he may have had in producing an adequate account of meaning is relatively insignificant in assessing his achievements. Indeed, as Jonathan Culler indicates, attempts to solve the problems of semantics have continued to prove intractable even during the past twenty years or so in which advances in all areas of linguistic study have been otherwise so successful. In *The Handbook of Contemporary Semantic Theory*, published in 1996, an essay on the state of play in semantics and natural language interpretation by Ruth M. Kempson may suggest a plausible explanation for this failure in that:

> Semantics as the study of meaning in natural languages, and pragmatics as the study of how utterances are interpreted, might seem to be one and the same study. Given that the meaning of an expression is the information that the expression conveys, and that interpretation by users

of the language is the retrieval of information from expressions, it may be hard to envisage that they could be separable.[9]

The notion of pragmatics arose among linguists in the 1930s as a supplement to the traditional linguistic categories of syntax (relations among signs) and semantics (relations of signs and meanings) to deal with a large set of theoretical anomalies. These anomalies often turned on the inconvenient fact that even properly formed sentences using ordinary words were often capable of bearing remarkably different meanings in different settings and contexts. A good example of the pragmatic difference that P. F. Strawson noted[10] between sentences and statements is that the sentence, "That lecture was simply excellent," when uttered by a university student in a certain setting, with a certain facial expression and with certain intonational flourishes, could be used to make an ironic *statement* whose meaning would be quite opposite to that borne by the same *sentence* in most other contexts. If meaning is importantly context-dependent, then traditional attempts to deal exhaustively with it in purely supra-contextual terms would indeed be misguided, hence Ruth Kempson's just call for conflating the two areas of study.

Another possibility would be to move the entire discussion of meaning to a more general level, for not only do words as signifiers, what linguists now call "lexemes," function as elements of meaning, but so too do intonational, gestural, and physiognomic elements participate in the pragmatic realization of meanings in actual contexts. In addition to these elements, sociolinguists now talk about "proxemic" elements in which the actual disposition of people's bodies in social space influences meaning. From this perspective, a fully adequate account of how words mean may simply not be possible exclusively in lexemic terms. If we are mistaken in viewing verbal formulae as equivalent to human language and if words are incapable of expressing all meanings all by themselves, we would have a fairly complete explanation for the chronic delay in formulating an adequate semantic theory in purely lexemic terms. Our tendency to view models of human communication as a congeries of discrete meaning systems where "language" and "nonverbal communication" are treated as logically independent may be at fault. Perhaps it would be more helpful to think of the units of meaningful communication not as "words" or "actions" but as "word-actions" blended and conjoined, sometimes verbally expressed, sometimes nonverbally, and often both. Compare, for example, the meaning of people disputing an academic point with that of people shouting in rage. In the first instance words are necessary; in the second, super-fluous. Sometimes, as in the meaning of intimates touching, words are simply impossible. Such an interactive account of word-actions would show why words in the ironic mode may, as we have already seen, pragmatically mean their opposites. If Ruth Kempson is right to call for the conflation of pragmatics and semantics, then perhaps it may not be seen as too impetuous to suggest considering still fur-ther meaningful mergers.

TOWARD MEANING WITHOUT PRESENCE

Just as there is no necessary reason to adopt *différance* simply be-cause Saussure's theory of meaning is flawed, there is no necessary reason to do so because Husserl's account may be seen as compara-bly flawed. Indeed no set of deconstructions, however ambitious, can ever show in principle that a genuinely informative theory of meaning is impossible. Indeed there enough evidence of produc-tive meaning in so many areas of human thought and action, pro-ductive meaning that does not depend upon an ultimately validat-ing presence, that we would be justified in placing the burden of proof with those who would argue the contrary. For notwithstand-ing contemporary preoccupations with relativism and indetermi-nacy, we do observe in all areas of human thought and action mean-ing and judgment grounded, if not in the ultimate presence of logos, at least in productive and publicly accountable ways. In seeking out better ways of finding scope for productive, if always ultimately provisional, agreement in judgments, it will be helpful to revisit the concept of the postmodern in the next chapter.

NOTES

1. Terry Eagleton, *The Illusions of Postmodernism* (Oxford: Blackwell, 1996), p. vii.

2. Ferdinand de Saussure, *Course in General Linguistics*, trans. Wade Baskin (Suffolk: Fontana/Collins, 1974), p. 120.

3. See Claude Lévi-Strauss, *Myth and Meaning* (Toronto: University of Toronto Press, 1978), pp. 12–13, and *Conversations with Claude Lévi-Strauss*, trans. Paula Wissing (Chicago: University of Chicago Press, 1991), p. 142, for a discussion of the mature structuralist conception of meaning. The crucial link to Kant is discussed in *Conversations*, p. 108.

4. Jacques Derrida, *Of Grammatology*, trans. G. C. Spivak (Baltimore: Johns Hopkins University Press, 1974), pp. 43–44.

5. Jacques Derrida, *Positions*, trans. Alan Bass (Chicago: University of Chicago Press, 1981), p. 28.

6. Ibid., p. 29.

7. Derrida, *Grammatology*, p. 158.

8. Jonathan Culler, introduction to *Course in General Linguistics* by Ferdinand de Saussure (Suffolk: Fontana/Collins, 1974), p. xxiv.

9. Ruth M. Kempson, "Semantics, Pragmatics, and Natural-Language Interpretation," in *The Handbook of Contemporary Semantic Theory*, ed. Shalom Lappin (Oxford: Blackwell, 1996), p. 561.

10. See P. F. Strawson, *Introduction to Logical Theory* (London: Methuen and Company, 1952).

3

Constructive Postmodernism

The seduction of High Modernity lay in its abstract neatness and theoretical simplicity: both of these features
blinded the successors of Descartes to the unavoidable
complexities of concrete human experience.

—Stephen Toulmin
Cosmopolis: The Hidden Agenda of Modernity

The deconstructive movement in postmodern cultural and literary
criticism has certainly embraced the complexity of human experience to which Stephen Toulmin alludes in the opening quotation,[1]
especially the complexity of interpretation and reading itself. In this
acceptance deconstruction returns criticism once again to an awareness of the complex environments of textual significance that, before the New Criticism of John Crowe Ransom and Cleanth Brooks
settled into orthodoxy, had always characterized the process of studying literary texts. In their own "high modern" pursuit of "neatness
and theoretical simplicity," the New Critics had eagerly abandoned
those historical, psychological, and social frameworks that had so
richly contextualized premodern literary criticism for strictly formal analyses of the text itself. The significance of texts was to be
found by these new, ontological critics embedded in the verbal materials of the autonomous text, and the differentials between literary and nonliterary texts were to be expressible elegantly in largely
linguistic terms. Limited to essentials, literary critics would come to

find, as artists and architects were discovering at about the same time, more in less.

In breaking the hold of High Modernity's "blinding" infatuation with reductive and essentialist explanations, deconstruction has had a very healthy influence on cultural studies and philosophy. The effects will not have been altogether salubrious, however, if in displacing the seductive charms of logocentrism, deconstruction has replaced one kind of procedurally fascinating dogma with another. Certainly, the equally compelling, even thrilling, allure of the trace among those ambivalent deconstructive meanings perpetually deferred in complex interrelationships can entice a newly liberated critic into a very heady mixture of analytical conceits. This phenomenon is particularly visible in the deconstructive criticism of the Yale School and is particularly ironic here given the fact that so much of the criticism of Paul de Man and his colleagues makes abundant use of the modernist text-in-itself procedural obsessions of the New Criticism it endeavors to supplant. Contrasting the work of a critic like Geoffrey Hartman, for example, before and after his exposure to Derrida shows how the constraints of the modern approach to literary studies may give way, perhaps too abundantly, to the free, relaxed play of critical intelligence. In his self-analytical reflections on the new interpretive tools, Hartman clearly finds the freedom to manipulate deconstructive exegetical strategies most exhilarating. He even finds the deconstructive critical process as worthwhile, creatively, as the artist's manipulation of aesthetic materials.[2]

In reading Derrida or de Man and Hartman, readers are often impressed with where the streams of critical consciousness may lead, but it is also fair to say that the same readers may also find many of the critical tributaries tedious, even at times self-indulgent and uninformative. The previous chapter attempted to show that however exciting and interesting succumbing to the deconstructive matrix of ambivalent meanings may be, it is not the only means of critical exploration available. In urging that the possibilities for more focused and deliberate investigations have not been eliminated by Derrida's conception of *différance*, and therefore remain intact, the previous chapter creates an opportunity now to provide an approach to meaning and rationality, which while clearly postmodern in its active embrace of uncertainty and the irreducible texture and complexity of human experience, is also quite distinct from the endemic ambivalences of deconstruction.

Stephen Toulmin's *Cosmopolis: The Hidden Agenda of Modernity*, from which the opening quotation is taken, is in part a comprehensive case in support of a such an approach. Toulmin, himself a student of Wittgenstein, has throughout his career studied the applications of his teacher's later work to the business of understanding meaning and the concept of human rationality. This chapter will present Toulmin's ideas, as well as those of his teacher and John Dewey, within the context of postmodern thinking; but the kind of postmodernism at work here is different in important ways from that previously discussed. For this reason and because Toulmin rightly sees much vagueness and some ambiguity in the term "postmodern," he is open in *Cosmopolis* to having his conception presented as part of a "new and distinctive 'post-modern'"[3] period or in terms of a late, far-sided phase of "modernity" itself. This chapter will take the first option, placing Toulmin's conception of rationality within the broad context of postmodernism. In so doing some important opportunities for constructive development in contemporary cultural studies will be identified.

Implicit in Toulmin's use of "modernity" rather than "modernism" in his title is a distinction that has sometimes confounded attempts to achieve conceptual clarity in respect of the meaning of the "postmodern." It has been already argued that a very important element of postmodern thought arose in direct, negative response to the products of modernism that dominated the arts and culture generally for much of the twentieth century. Exemplified in Toulmin's *Cosmopolis*, however, there is another, related meaning of the postmodern to be developed. Among philosophers like John Dewey, Toulmin, and Toulmin's own teacher, Ludwig Wittgenstein, it is possible to discern a particular perspective on the postmodern that may be distinguished in a more temperate, and certainly more deliberate, rejection of a specifically "modern" conception of rationality. This modern conception, securely grounded in the possibility of certainty, is based upon the logically inexorable model of mathematics. In this case, however, the relevant "modern" point of view that *these* postmodern philosophers reject is approximately four hundred years old.

Deconstructive postmodernism, paradigmatically expressed in the work of Jacques Derrida, may, of course, be characterized by its focused opposition to philosophically traditional forms of rational certainty as well as to the more general foundational preoccupations of twentieth-century modernism. Although the terminology and methodology of deconstructive analysis tempts us to see deconstructive postmodernism in predominantly negative terms, it is good to remember that in aiming to expose the chronic uncertainties that must inhabit any grounded system of thought, a deconstructive critic is also aiming to liberate thinking and writing in pursuit of innovative and provocative lines of inquiry. But since the view of meaning that inhabits these investigations makes, in their own terms, the possibility of consolidating and refining their purposes and products very problematic, if not impossible, it is easy to see why proponents of systematic and cumulatively productive cultural studies find deconstructive postmodernism so antagonistically relativistic.

If we use the term "deconstructive postmodernism" to refer specifically to those postmodern writers and critics who connect most naturally to the exegetical strategies of Derrida, then we open the possibility of contrastively regarding a philosopher like Dewey or Wittgenstein, who embraces uncertainty positively and productively, as "constructively" postmodern. What is being called here "constructive postmodernism" most importantly has not abandoned the effort to improve comprehensive, systematic, and epistemologically efficacious explanatory and justificatory frameworks, even though philosophers similarly situated conceptually to Dewey, like Stephen Toulmin and, before him, Wittgenstein, would make much more modest claims about the possibilities of grounding these frameworks in ultimately secure foundational principles. As Toulmin has written, whether we choose to see this approach to uncertainty as a new phase of Modernity "or as a new and distinctive 'post-modern' phase,"[4] constructive postmodernism rejects the model of rationality that is the cornerstone of modern philosophical (and scientific) thought for one that is more relevant to the actual uses of reason in making productive decisions. But unlike deconstructive postmodern critiques that yield to the lure of Derrida's traces, the constructive postmodern approach seeks to achieve plateaus of productive stability in our inquiries and hence to enhance the possibilities for cumulative and meaningful discourse in cultural studies.

It may seem odd to consider thinkers like Dewey and Wittgenstein already well known within other descriptive categories as essentially postmodern, but it may be hoped that seeing them in this light might startle us into realizing that the most epistemologically vexatious revelations of so many deconstructive analyses are by no means novel discoveries of the deconstructive process and that notwithstanding the strong sentiments expressed by many deconstructive postmodernists to the contrary, it *is* possible to work cooperatively, cumulatively, and meaningfully within these constraints. Dewey shows us most clearly that the hope for intellectual progress need not be thrown out with the bathwater of falsely grounded certainty. Indeed, for Dewey actively embracing uncertainty is an opportunity to reconstruct the very enterprise of philosophical inquiry on more plausible naturalistic footings:

> Any philosophy that in its quest for certainty ignores the reality of the uncertain in the ongoing processes of nature denies the conditions out of which it arises. The attempt to include all that is doubtful within the fixed grasp of that which is theoretically certain is committed to insincerity and evasion, and in consequence will have the stigmata of internal contradiction.[5]

Here in Dewey's *Quest for Certainty* is the essence of deconstruction without the pyrotechnics, and the virtually complete anticipation of the binary discoveries that have been so recently celebrated in cultural studies. As Dewey notes so tellingly, "Every such philosophy is marked at some point by a division of its subject-matter into the truly real and the merely apparent, a subject and an object, a physical and a mental, an ideal and an actual, that have nothing to do with one another, save in some mode which is so mysterious as to create an insoluble problem."[6] Unlike Derrida, who views the production of such binary systems as an unavoidable and mischievous corruption of systematic thought by an antic and imperious *archi-écriture*, Dewey simply acknowledges this to be a mistaken attempt to separate thinking from experience.

CARTESIAN RATIONALITY

Although it would be foolish to try to identify a date on which either ancient or medieval philosophy commenced, one could quite plausibly point to November 10, 1619, as the birthdate of modern philosophy, for it was on that date that a very young René Descartes, passing a solitary and reflective day in a warm room in Germany, began a project that would revolutionize systematic thought and, in its pursuit of mathematically certain principles of rationality, initiate the modern age. Descartes gives us the specific products of that thoughtful day in the *Discourse on the Method*, a work that inaugurates the conception of rationality that has dominated modern philosophical and scientific thinking since that time. At the core of this conception of rationality is the conviction that reason must, as the extended title of the *Discourse* indicates, be "rightly conducted" if it is to be successful in establishing truth "in the field of science."[7] As a very successful student in the famous Royal College at La Flèche, Descartes had enjoyed abundant opportunities to observe the nimble dexterity of reason, as the Jesuit masters worked their way through the college's medieval curriculum. The Scholastic curriculum was effectively based on the medieval instructional heuristic of the disputation. Subtle points of philosophy or theology would be routinely tested by a vigorous intellectual contest of *pro versus contra*, with the student's ultimate academic credibility evaluated on his disputational skills.

Notwithstanding the application of "the most outstanding minds" to this argumentative process over centuries of effort, the student Descartes had observed that philosophical reasoning had not produced anything "which is not in dispute and consequently doubtful and uncertain."[8] Having effectively already "deconstructed" the "very superb and magnificent palaces built only on mud and sand"[9] as a schoolboy, Descartes contrasted the ambivalence and uncertainty of these paradigms of ancient and medieval philosophy with the logical purity and ideal demonstrability of mathematical, especially geometrical, proofs: "I was especially pleased with mathematics, because of the certainty and self-evidence of its proofs . . . [but] I was astonished that nothing more noble had been built on so firm and solid a foundation."[10]

The defining, modern move Descartes made in that warm room in 1619 was to use the model of mathematics "rightly" to conduct or discipline human rationality. The philosophical and scientific program that ultimately emerged sought to conduct the reason using four principal rules.[11] First, modeled on the privileged position foundational postulates have in geometry, Descartes vowed "never to accept anything as true unless I recognized it to be certainly and evidently such." Likewise following the kind of analysis undertaken in geometric demonstrations, "the second was to divide each of the difficulties which I encountered into as many parts as possible, and as might be required for an easier solution." Similarly, the third rule requires proceeding in a orderly and systematic fashion, progressing from "things which were simplest and easiest to understand, and gradually moving toward more complex knowledge." Finally, Descartes promises in the *Discourse on the Method* to be so careful and comprehensive in his investigations "that I would be certain that nothing was omitted." Thus the modern conception of rationality, initiated by Descartes, is held to be capable of establishing certain knowledge with conclusive evidentiary foundations. Much of modern philosophy has been concerned to discover the conditions necessary for such certain knowledge to be possible.

DEWEY'S INSTRUMENTALISM

John Dewey's productive engagement of uncertainty may be taken as a fundamental repudiation of this Cartesian model of rationality as well as a challenge to the substance and style of the deconstructive rejection of the same model. Dewey began, as we have already seen, with the *fact* of uncertainty in nature; his strategy for dealing with this unavoidable fact is to recognize straightaway that in spite of it we have succeeded in developing highly efficacious ways of coping productively with very problematic environments and have achieved progressively more efficacious plateaus of relative stability in the process. Accounting for these successes and understanding how the strategies implicit in their success may be consolidated and strengthened is the subject-matter of his unique form of naturalistic empiricism. Dewey emphasizes the centrality of experience in coming to terms with the problems addressed in the history of conventional philosophical inquiry, but he firmly rejects the distorted emphasis on ideas and cognition in all forms of philosophical idealism. In rejecting the epistemological primacy of ideas, however, Dewey also rejects, with equal fervor, the primacy of experience in traditional British empiricism. The metaphysical systems of Bradley and McTaggart discussed earlier in this study and the logical atomism of Russell and Wittgenstein may be seen as exemplars of both views which Dewey is quick to reject. If Bradley's insistence on the centrality of mind is mistaken, Dewey insists, so too is the logical empiricists' spectator theory of knowledge. Experience for Dewey cannot simply be a projection of mind, nor can it simply be conceived as a structured set of passive cognitive opportunities awaiting the informing influence of natural perceptions. For Dewey both models, however capable each one might be for generating detailed and coherent accounts of experience, were to be rejected on grounds of relevance to the actualities of experience and in favor of a richly textured, biologically grounded, organic account.

Experience, for Dewey, arises in the interaction of a live creature and its environment. In Dewey the felt quality of experience as human beings actually interact with their environing conditions, is a central feature. Dewey held that this pervasive quality of experience results from the integral participation in experience of *what we might contextually otherwise refer to as* emotional quality, aesthetic quality, and cognition. While conventional philosophy draws fundamental distinctions among emotion, aesthetic quality, and cognition, Dewey urges that we reach behind these abstract distinctions for the natural rhythm and flow of experience and recognize that although these concepts may be used in contextually useful ways, they should always be understood nonreductively as representing emphases within experiential phenomena rather than fully discrete phenomena in and of themselves. One of the reasons that conventional philosophers are sometimes so impatient with Dewey, therefore, is that they perceive in the abandonment of the intellectual security of these abstractions a conceptually retrograde development. Another reason that Dewey is so difficult to grasp is that he is asking that we temporarily put these conceptual distinctions out of gear even though they have come to function effectively for us as basic units of thought, so that we might recover the less differentiated awareness of experience out of which these abstractions have arisen.

In this integrated conception of experience, its aesthetic aspect plays a fundamental role; indeed, it might be argued that the aesthetic dimension of experience is at the very core of Dewey's instrumentalism. The complete act of thought, that is Dewey's model of problem solving and thereby of the development of knowledge, has an aesthetic structure. Thought is initially provoked by a disequilibrium in environing conditions that is initially felt and then resolved, often through the explicit application of cognitive tools, in a new recovery of equilibrium through growth. This recovery of equilibrium is also felt, but now pleasurably as a consummation, a highly gratifying feeling of completeness and purposeful integrity. Thus for Dewey the trajectory of this act of thought, of the structure of inquiry itself, is fundamentally aesthetic, with growth resulting from the development of a new, tested strategy for coping productively with an environmental challenge or problem. The dynamics of the aesthetic dimension of successful inquiry may be found developed in great detail in Dewey's *Art as Experience*, while the corresponding examination of the structure of inquiry itself is examined in comparable detail in Dewey's *Logic: The Theory of Inquiry*. In a very important sense, art, for Dewey, is the engine of inquiry.

In Dewey's *Logic*, inquiry is treated in functional and situational terms rather than in the formal terms normally associated with this subject matter. Logic *is* the theory of inquiry, in which human beings as sentient beings are able to respond to challenges in environing conditions both dispositionally or viscerally and through the application and enhancement of linguistically and conceptually mediated, culturally achieved and learned conceptual tools. In keeping with his acceptance of the fact of uncertainty in nature, Dewey's conception of inquiry presents conclusions and findings as always provisional, with "warranted assertability" rather than certain truth providing the goal or product of successful inquiry. In his famous definition of inquiry, Dewey makes clear both the organic and the aesthetic dimensions of his view of logic. "Inquiry," writes Dewey, "is the controlled or directed transformation of an indeterminate situation into one that is so determinate in its constituent distinctions and relations as to convert the elements of the original situation into a unified whole."[12]

Simply put, when we become viscerally aware of an anomaly in our environing conditions (whether the environment in question is physical, social, or symbolic), this novel element in the situation presents a problem or an obstacle to further experience, in that previously acquired and tested strategies for working through problematic situations are not now seen as applicable. If the problem is to be taken up, then we must try to change or enhance the set of strategies available so that the problem may be handled successfully. Engaging a problem is therefore stressful in that it represents an implicit acknowledgment of vulnerability. If the problem is engaged, an active application of strategies and conceptual tools is brought to bear on the problem. If the situational experiential materials are reconfigured in such a way that the anomaly is resolved and the prior unity is recovered, the problem is solved and we have *grown* in solving it. Dewey uses the word "growth" because it signifies a net gain in the set of problem-solving strategies available to us, such that when comparable situations to the one just resolved are encountered in future, there will be no need for further stress and our future vulnerability to a whole set of challenges in environing conditions will have been significantly reduced. Inasmuch as such growth represents increased efficacy, it is not surprising that nature rewards us with feelings of satisfaction and gratification when we realize that we have solved a significant problem.

Dewey makes a special point in directing us to read "situation" in the definition of "inquiry" quoted earlier within the context of his prior discussion of that term in the *Logic*. In keeping with the integrated conception of experience already discussed here, situations are to be understood in the following way. "What is designated by the word 'situation' is *not* a single object or event or set of objects and events. For we never experience nor form judgments about objects and events in isolation, but only in connection with a contextual whole. This latter is what is called a 'situation.'"[13]

In experience what we have come to represent as specific objects, for instance, do not function discretely at all:

> In actual experience, there is never any . . . isolated singular object or event; *an* object is always a special part, phase, or aspect, of an environing experienced world—a situation. The singular object stands out conspicuously because of its especially focal and crucial position at a given time in determination of some problem of use or enjoyment which the *total* complex environment presents. There is always a *field* in which observation of *this* or *that* object or event occurs. [14]

Using experiential phenomena "cognitively," as singular "objects" in inquiry, results inevitably in distortions that make the goal of certainty impossible to realize. But these imperfect, fallible representations may still be used productively in the various contexts of inquiry. The propensity to form these symbolically mediated representations is, in fact, an important part of our evolutionary strategy. Intervening strategically within the act of thought or problem solving presumes identifying discrete "elements" of experience and seeking to establish "causal" links among them. "Controlling and directing inquiry" meaningfully presumes representation, but, of course, representation presumes selection and inevitable distortion. Even though such selection ultimately must misrepresent the organic nature of human situations, this propensity and capability have thus far worked well instrumentally for us, sometimes with wonderfully efficacious results. The use of such representations may be seen as an important part of who and what we are as a species. The concepts and ideas we routinely use efficaciously as tools of thought are and must be treated by us in practice as having direct phenomenal significance, even if they ultimately only represent a very useful delusion.

One way of emphasizing the difference between Derrida's ambivalent response to uncertainty and Dewey's constructive engagement of this fact is to compare Derrida's *archi-écriture* with Dewey's notion of ordinary experience. *Archi-écriture* with its perpetual deferrals of *différance* within a complex economy of traces and Dewey's notion of ordinary experience are interestingly both ungrounded and inchoate. Dewey describes ordinary experience in *Art as Experience* as characterized by "distraction and dispersion,"[15] qualities that equally characterize the multifarious pathways of Derrida's traces in the everything-that-is-the-text, but unlike Derrida's perpetually deferred meanings, Dewey's interactive pathways of dispersion may suddenly focus quite dramatically. "Under conditions of resistance and conflict," Dewey writes, "aspects and elements of the self and the world that are implicated in this interaction qualify experience with emotions and ideas so that conscious intent emerges."[16] If the problem posed in this resistance or conflict is taken up, ideas and meanings are brought directly and as clearly as possible to bear on the matter at hand. The ordinary experiential rhythms of dispersion and distraction are brought abruptly to a halt, and whatever lure that traces may possess is similarly brought quickly to heel so that the problem, and its inherent indeterminacies, may be resolved. A successfully completed act of thought may not result in infallible results, of course, but neither may it be seen as arbitrary or capricious. The efficacy of the specific meanings that have functioned productively as tools in this act have been tested and have provisionally passed the test.

WITTGENSTEINIAN COMPLEXITIES

Recalling the discussion of Russell and the early Wittgenstein in Chapter One illustrates the pervasiveness in traditional philosophical inquiry of the very model of logic and rationality Dewey rejects so emphatically. Whether one takes the Cartesian *cogito* and its subsequent clear and distinct ideas as the self-evident postulates or the "facts in relations" pressing themselves ineluctably on the mind in logical empiricism, the same, neomathematical, rational locus of inquiry is present in both. But suppose knowing and meaning as human activities are more complexly entangled in the thickets of human judgment, as Dewey and the later work of Wittgenstein came to demonstrate, than modern philosophy can recognize. Suppose the ways in which human beings actually use language productively defy reduction into logically simple and precisely manipulatable propositional categories. Toward the end of Chapter One it was shown how such ideas were instrumental in Wittgenstein's thinking as he began systematically to doubt the central tenets of his own *Tractatus Logico-Philosophicus*, and in his second career at Cambridge relentlessly to deconstruct his own masterpiece of modern (and modernist) philosophy.

The products of this self-criticism were published after his death as the *Philosophical Investigations*. Both the method and conclusions of the demonstrations in this work are clearly postmodern in their substance and style. In place of the hierarchically numbered and subordinated tiers of rigorously interconnected propositions to be found in the *Tractatus*, the *Investigations* are presented as thematically linked remarks; in place of the neat isomorphism of thought, word, and object in the first book, the second aims to show how that picture held us *captive*. Through a variety of examples and counterexamples of language productively and nonproductively in use, Wittgenstein demonstrates that even though we often *believe* we can actually trace the outline of a thing's true nature, we are simply tracing the frame within which we see it. Wittgenstein shows that when we look at the world through language, we see not facts so much as aspects of ourselves, our common (i.e., shared) sense, representations of our own purposes, interests, and concerns—our forms of life; or, of more specialized forms of inquiry as expressed more systematically in theories, views, orientations. Hence if we wish to gain understanding of the meaning of a word, we should look to the use, for it is in its use that the deep cultural or disciplinary interests that the word has come to mark out may be appreciated. The relationship between meaning and the complex social activities in which it is achieved is central, with behavioral cues functioning closely with symbolic ones.

What reasons did Wittgenstein have for abandoning the view of the *Tractatus* and developing this new view of language? First, one fundamental presumption of the *Tractatus* held that the basic components of linguistic meaning and the world were reducible to simple basic terms. This position Wittgenstein came to consider untenable. Wittgenstein questions the very intelligibility of inquiring into such simple component ingredients.

> But what are the simple constituent parts of which reality is composed?—What are the simple constituent parts of a chair?—The bits of wood of which it is made? Or the molecules, or the atoms?—"Simple" means: not composite. And here the point is: in what sense "composite"? It makes no sense at all to speak absolutely of the "simple parts of a chair."[17]

Equally important, the essential link between these allegedly simple constituents and language was ostension. But did not the very activity of pointing itself presuppose a network of shared judgments and conventions? Could pointing have any significance independent of the cultural context in which one came to understand what to make of that activity? Pointing to a red book while shouting "red" could not fix the meaning *all by itself*. Why, for instance, should one attend to the color of the book? Why not to its shape, or position, or composition?[18]

Moreover is there any *necessary* reason that the eyes should follow the hand to the finger and then to the object? Why not the other direction? Could we not imagine a successful human culture in which what *we* should describe as pointing had a very different significance? "The arrow points only in the application that a living being makes of it."[19] Ostension, the crucial link to establish significance between word and object in Wittgenstein's earlier view, *since it itself requires human conventions in order to be meaningful*, plainly could not "produce" meaning.

Meaning in the postmodern *Investigations* is certainly not part of a logico-mathematical rational calculus, but a complex socially achieved tool steeped in the variegated textures of language games and forms of life, enabled by the agreements in judgments productive concept users conventionally make; or as Stephen Toulmin puts it:

> For the later Wittgenstein . . . the "meaning" of any utterance is determined by the rule-conforming, symbol-using activities ("language games") within which the expressions in question are conventionally put to use; and these symbol-using activities in turn draw their significance from

the broader patterns of activities (or "forms of life") in which they are embedded and of which they are a constituent element.[20]

STEPHEN TOULMIN'S CONTRIBUTIONS

Toulmin was a student of Wittgenstein's at Cambridge and has done much in the intervening decades to explain and, in some important ways, to extend the reach of his teacher's demonstrations in respect of engaging constructively the challenges to meaning and knowing implicit in Wittgenstein's abandonment of the traditional modern framework for dealing with these issues. Toulmin's strategy has been to study carefully the social and psychological contexts within which purposeful human activities achieve meaning and to explore the impact such understanding may have on the concept of "concept" itself. This sensitivity to the ways in which the empirical mingles with the conceptual has caused Toulmin to be very wary of any strict distinction between the analytic, that which philosophers maintain can be understood independently of experience, and the experientially discoverable synthetic. Both the social genealogy of concepts and their psychological genesis in individuals are relevant to what our concepts have meant, the social choices they have come to embody, and the complex ways in which they enable meaningful communication among us to occur. Toulmin has written many books but the work he did in the 1970s on conceptual change, culminating in *Human Understanding: The Collective Use and Evolution of Concepts*, is of most direct relevance to the question of conceptual grasp. A close, critical reading of a published debate on these problems from this period of Toulmin's work, between Toulmin and the analytic philosopher D. W. Hamlyn, will help bring the pertinent issues clearly into focus.

Hamlyn's philosophically modern or "fixed" view of meaning treats conceptual questions as completely distinct from questions about our experience in and of the world. In principle we seek to determine the answer to an empirical question in what the world shows, while answers to conceptual questions can be determined simply by reflecting carefully and systematically on the meanings of the key concepts at work in the questions themselves. This is a view of meaning that Descartes would find most agreeable. The philosophically or constructively postmodern view of meaning, on the other hand, would see a necessary interplay between the genesis of concepts historically and psychologically and the process of making further choices respecting the future possibilities of productive meaning. While the fixed view focuses on the logical status of concepts as autonomous expressions of meaning, the process view attends to the genesis of concepts historically, the development of concepts in individuals, and the possibilities of meaning with regard to empirical and theoretical concerns. On the fixed view the central question to be pursued in the analysis of concepts is: What do we mean by X? On the constructively postmodern view the question becomes: What is there for us to mean by X? The task of analysis on the fixed view is clarificatory and reportive, while on the process view, it is positive and constructive.

WHAT IS THERE FOR US TO MEAN BY MEANING?

The two papers to be examined are D. W. Hamlyn's "Epistemology and Conceptual Development" and Stephen Toulmin's "The Concept of 'Stages' in Psychological Development." Hamlyn's essay is largely pessimistic about the possibility of philosophically informative interaction across the analytic/synthetic divide. The central purpose of Hamlyn's paper is to argue that epistemological and conceptual concerns are necessarily independent of questions concerning the genesis of concepts and knowledge. Hamlyn is quick to propose a dividing line between his and Toulmin's view of concepts. Hamlyn claims that, unlike Toulmin, he believes that questions concerning what is involved in having a concept can be discussed "illuminatingly" and independently from considering more psychologically pertinent concerns respecting the acquisition of that concept and related concepts. Toulmin, on the other hand, would assert that the opposite is the case and that cooperative inquiries among philosophers and psychologists are not only desirable but necessary.

Hamlyn's initial view of the debate, however, does not accurately capture the thrust of Toulmin's position. Toulmin does not deny the fact that philosophers routinely and independently discuss the question of what it is to have a concept *illuminatingly*; what he denies is that the philosopher can do so *exhaustively* without recourse to information on the genesis of the concepts in question. Interestingly, Hamlyn is not claiming that cooperative work by philosophers and psychologists is misguided or pointless (as some philosophers might impatiently maintain) but that there is a large gap between desirability and necessity. Indeed, Hamlyn later acknowledges, following Wittgenstein, "It is clear enough that light *can* be cast on a given concept by asking how it is typically acquired; the question is whether an understanding of what it is to have that concept *requires* us to ask how it is typically acquired."[21] It will, therefore, be useful in this discussion to distinguish between the necessity thesis (Toulmin's) and the desirability thesis (Hamlyn's) in an attempt to isolate the implications that the necessity thesis will have for postmodern conceptual analysis.

Hamlyn offers three related arguments against the necessity thesis as argued in Toulmin's "Concepts and the Explanation of Human Behavior." These arguments will be critically considered in turn. First, Hamlyn argues that there is no *one* way in which a given concept is acquired, that concepts are acquired in various ways depending on the specific developmental histories of individual concept-users. As such, "we cannot insist that they do not have the concept unless they have acquired it in some particular way."[22] The force of this argument resides presumably in the assumption that Toulmin is holding something accidental (a *particular* way of acquiring a concept) to be necessary and has, therefore, lapsed into incoherence. But this assumption is mistaken. Toulmin may consistently hold that it is *general information* regarding the genesis of a concept that is necessary to our understanding fully the contours of that concept (or, as Hamlyn himself put it above, how a concept is *typically* acquired), without being committed to any particular way of acquiring that concept. Imperfect information is better than no information at all, and such imperfect information (structured as it is from within the theoretical framework within which it is garnered) may well be in the form of relevant generalizations from developmental psychology. A further difficulty in Hamlyn's first argument may be expressed in the following questions: Assuming concepts are learned, just *how* widely may the ways of acquiring, say, the concept of book vary before we become reluctant to insist that it is the same concept of book at all? May the rare book dealer be said to have the same concept of book as the average university student?

Hamlyn's second argument is an attack on Toulmin's position that the justification of the necessity thesis finds support in the fact that the scientific criteria for recognizing when any process is completed cannot be stipulated in advance of researching the actual course of the process. To make such a move in connection with the business of conceptual grasp, claims Hamlyn, is surely to beg the question, in that it assumes that "we have the right to speak of a process" in this "putatively parallel question."[23] In this Hamlyn is correct. The charge of question begging is true, but trivially so insofar as the process/product interdependency is *central* to the postmodern epistemological reconstruction Toulmin is advocating. As such, as Stephen C. Pepper argued in his *World Hypotheses*, a charge of question begging in such an intertheoretical dispute does not take us very far. The acceptability or unacceptability of the process view must ultimately be assessed on its overall adequacy as a theory of knowledge and of conceptual change.

Hamlyn further attacks the process view by asserting that "there might well be many processes of acquiring a given concept or even none at all . . . [and] if that is so, how can an understanding of what it is to have grasped a concept presuppose as a matter of necessity an understanding of the process of acquiring it?"[24] The salient point here, of course, is the possibility of innate concepts. The appropriate countermove would be that if concepts were innate we should be dealing with a different notion of "concept" from the one implicit in Toulmin. Hence, Toulmin's view may be wrong in whole or in part if some or all concepts are shown to be innate, but there would still be no logical inconsistency in the process view as Hamlyn implies.

The argument against the process view moves to a more general level in Hamlyn's next challenge. A counter-example is produced as an argument against the very idea of a product-process interdependency. Hamlyn asks whether the criteria involved in determining when a journey has been concluded necessarily involve data respecting the course of that journey. "Surely," he writes, "I may know what it is to have arrived somewhere without any knowledge of the actual journey."[25] This is a significant move, but Hamlyn's case is not as strong as it might be. How would one know that a *journey* had been completed without knowledge of that journey? The extent of what it means to have completed that journey will depend upon the extent of our knowledge of that journey. The point Hamlyn wants to make is that one could know what it means to be somewhere without any knowledge of the means by which one arrived there. But this, of course, is precisely what is at issue. Toulmin's point, and the one that needs to be addressed (in terms of Hamlyn's counter-example) is whether our notions of what it means to be somewhere will be in part determined by what it has taken us to get there—individually in terms of the acquisition of the given concept and collectively in terms of the cultural history that has achieved that concept.

The third principal argument that Hamlyn offers attacks the process-product interdependency view from an Aristotelian angle. Hamlyn argues that only with a knowledge of the criteria for what it is to have a concept of "x" can we know what will count toward acquiring it. Hence Toulmin has put his genetic cart before the horse. It is on this point that the debate turns, for it is here we get a picture of Hamlyn's view of concepts and that of the modern analytical philosophy he may be taken to represent. The view of concepts implicit in Hamlyn's argument is that of the concept neatly fixed in the linguistic ether of the forms of knowledge and forms of understanding. Concepts are final and complete entities like the concept "red," an understanding of which is characterized by Hamlyn in the following way: "a full understanding of what red is brings along with it a nexus of understanding of other things, and one cannot be said fully to understand it until one understands that whole nexus."[26] This sort of characterization raises the question of whether it is ever possible fully to understand anything at all. Just how many things about "red" are necessary to full understanding? If all red-related facts and things are necessary, if complete mastery of the nexus of related understandings is required, and if the nexus of understanding is an ongoing enterprise, then perhaps no one ever fully understands anything. If so, then it is not possible to understand fully what is meant by "Hand me the red book that is on the shelf, please," since it is not possible to understand the complete nexus of understanding that color theorists, to say nothing about visual artists, shall ultimately cast upon the concept "red." This is, of course, absurd. We do understand the sentence fully. The conventional modern position on concepts leads one to the absurd conclusions suggested, if pushed.

THE "PROCESS" VIEW

Toulmin's "The Concept of 'Stages' in Developmental Psychology," which develops an alternative to the modern or fixed view, begins with a discussion of two important epistemological "oversimplifications" First, what Toulmin appropriately calls the Cartesian oversimplification entails that one must begin any inquiry by giving clear formulations and explicit analyses of his concepts before doing anything else. The Baconian oversimplification, on the other hand, holds that concepts and generalizations must be allowed to generate themselves freely from uninterpreted data. Toulmin holds that each view incorporates an important half-truth about the categories of empirical inquiry, but that either view alone is insufficient. His central question concerns the extent to which the products of learning or knowledge can be sufficiently understood prior to discovering the nature of the process of coming-to-know. In an attempt to sort out the problems involved in satisfactorily answering these questions, Toulmin first considers a potential solution. Hamlyn would hold that conceptual questions are always logically prior to empirical questions, hence the very notion of a *genetic* epistemology, one that maintains some form of the "process" thesis, is by its very nature incoherent. Toulmin argues that this is a species of the Cartesian oversimplification. The difficulties in maintaining such a rigid analytic/synthetic distinction are revealed in a family of cases, of which the concept of "curing" is a good example. The notion of "curing" a disease is, of course, logically prior to "treating" it, but Toulmin argues quite persuasively that what counts as a cure for a newly identified disease will develop gradually as the medical interventions proceed. At first the cure will simply involve procedures for ameliorating the most vexacious symptoms of the ailment, but as a clinical history of specific cases emerges and new targets for treatment are identified, the meaning of a cure for this disease will also progressively develop. This is a good example of the analytic-synthetic interpenetration central to Toulmin's process view: The possibilities of meaning will in part be determined by the status of our relevant empirical knowledge.

Toulmin discusses a second approach aimed at resolving the relationship between process and product with which his discussion commenced. Now to be scrutinized is the program of atheoretical psychologists who claim that if we wish to understand what it is to know, then we should approach children we are coming to know with a candid eye—one not colored by preconception—and then make suitable generalizations. That this view lapses into the Baconian oversimplification is readily seen, for "in this case, we can say nothing about the concepts of *learning* and *knowledge*, except what our detailed psychological observations warrant. Learning will now be just a phase that children go through—like teenage rebellion—and knowledge will be something they 'come out in'—like acne."[27]

Toulmin's resolution is to pass between the horns of his dilemma by proposing a middle way in which "the better we understand the course taken by *learning* the more precise an analysis we can give of the *knowledge* which is its outcome. (In this respect, 'knowing' stands to learning and studying as 'health' does to curing and treating.)"[28] It is with the development and defense of such a middle way that much of the rest of the paper is concerned. In support of the interdependency or "process" view, Toulmin argues that while it is possible formally to distinguish "analytic" from "synthetic" as terms it is impossible to separate them in application, offering both historical and philosophical arguments in support of his thesis. How else in the development of human thought have conceptual questions been settled except in light of empirical experiences? In this regard the crucial role played by Galileo's rolling-ball experiment in determining what was to be meant by "acceleration" (Galileo was uncertain as to whether acceleration should be defined with respect to distance or to time), the conceptual-cum-empirical analysis of "force" in Newton, and Einstein's work on "simultaneity" are reviewed. In each case, "where the concepts of a science are changing . . . the crucial questions are never purely empirical ('What *is the case* about X?') nor are they ever purely analytical ('What do we *already mean* by X?'). They are always . . . a 'blend' of the conceptual and the empirical ('What *is there for one to mean* by X?')."[29] An excellent contemporary example is the debate that has sprung up over the concept of "death" as a result of the development of artificial life-maintenance technology, as such technological possibilities cause us to reconsider the possibilities of meaning for death itself. With such a range of examples now in hand, Toulmin is in a position to formulate the crux of the disagreement between himself and Hamlyn, between the modern and constructively postmodern way of thinking: "I claim that 'learning' and 'knowing' are correlative terms, in the same general way as 'treating' and 'curing,' or 'living' and 'dying'; but he denies this."[30]

MEANING PRODUCTIVELY

In this regard Toulmin is very close to the conception of a concept demonstrated in Wittgenstein's *Philosophical Investigations*. While more powerful a conception than the fixed one, it is admittedly less tidy. To have a concept, on this view, is to have been initiated into a range of activities, or parts or aspects of such a range, in which meaning inheres in what the concept enables participants in the activities to do. It is to this depth grammar that Wittgenstein is referring in claiming that the meaning is the "use," not the surface (lexical) grammar that has so occupied ordinary language philosophers. What people do with a concept is in important ways dependent upon the collective nature of the activity (the interests, purposes, and concerns it reflects) and the individual's proficiency in the activity (just how well she or he has caught on); hence, meaning is not "fixed" across all people and all activities. To the extent that activities share strands of similarities, that is, what Wittgenstein calls "family resemblances," the meaning will also have strands of similarities: "And the strength of the thread does not reside in the fact that some one fiber runs through its whole length, but in the overlapping of many fibers."[31]

Meanings and the contours of concepts are variegated. The fabric of our ways of living in the world has a history but it is also continually being woven—with many varieties of pattern and stitch to accommodate the many uses we may have for our cloth. Surveying the richness of our activities, "we see a complicated network of similarities overlapping and criss-crossing: sometimes overall similarities, sometimes similarities of detail."[32]

Just as the activities of human beings are complex and multifarious, so, too, are the criteria for having a concept, as Toulmin properly insists, complex and context-dependent. If we are interested in representing some aspect of meaning, we must attend to some specific activity or activities and attempt to discover how the concept works and has come to work for its users in context. These contexts, the contexts of Wittgenstein's language games and forms of life, are *social*, hence the connection of Saussure's unified sign to the social structure of language discussed in the last chapter may now be seen significantly to have anticipated Wittgenstein's position. But implicit in the complexity of Wittgenstein's account of "following a rule" and explicit in Toulmin's process view of conceptual grasp lies the insight that a concept is a *variable* range of agreements in judgments respecting the use of an expression in a language game and that its efficacy results not from there being any essential commonalty to the ideas any or all of the concept-users may have formed respecting the concept in question but rather from the variably productive conformity of their uses of the expression.

Developing this line a bit further would indicate that a concept represents a group's consolidation for a time of a meaningful way to accommodate what it takes to be its interests. As interest groups collectively pursue their specialized ends, the requisite degree of conformity among the judgments of proficient concept-users increases and criteria for such newly specialized concepts become much more explicit. In *Human Understanding*, Toulmin seemed poised to use these collective interests or disciplinary ideals to help clarify the process of theoretical or conceptual change in subject areas like science, but important public debates on the uses of science and the new technologies it enabled, like recombinant DNA and fetal tissue use, caused him to reflect on the more complex underlying normative structures that operate at the deepest levels of culture and society. It became more difficult to conceive theoretical or disciplinary questions simply as such, and Toulmin's work began to move toward greater contextualization of conceptual and moral questions, greater appreciation of the situational complexity of working through these questions, and an increased skepticism about solving particular problems in general terms.

JURISPRUDENTIAL RATIONALITY

In seeking out exemplars of productive engagement and disposition of complex particular cases, Toulmin and Albert R. Jonsen looked systematically at the protocols of casuistry, a form of practical moral reasoning that reached its peak in the church between 1550 and 1650. In *The Abuse of Casuistry*, Toulmin and Jonsen set out a distinction between "two very different accounts of ethics and morality: one that seeks eternal, invariable principles, the practical implications of which can be free of exceptions or qualifications, and another, which pays closest attention to the specific details of particular moral cases and circumstances."[33]

The latter account, which resonates quite clearly with postmodern concerns about complexity and certainty, constructively opens the door to productive engagement of normative problems by shifting our attention from establishing general, universally applicable, and unchanging systems of propositional value theory toward the admittedly less fastidious but ultimately more defensible business of sorting out *reasonable* solutions to complex questions of value.

This casuitical or "case" approach to value or normative questions in his collaboration with Jonsen connected directly with earlier work Toulmin had done on logical theory. In *The Uses of Argument*, published in 1964, Toulmin had attacked the very core of the modern, Cartesian conception of rationality by offering an alternative account of the nature and scope of logic. In that work, the decidedly modern preoccupation with logic as a science that seeks to understand comprehensively the system of truths, governing logical relations was seen to be most completely realized in the work of Rudolph Carnap, in which "the implicit model for logic is . . . to be neither an explanatory science nor a technology, but rather pure mathematics."[34] This conception of logic may in turn be seen to be the consummation of the modern agenda for philosophy and science inaugurated by Descartes in that heated room in 1619, for here a mathematically modeled logic becomes the very means of all genuinely rational processes. By pursuing his investigation of logic through logical practice rather than logical theory, however, Toulmin demonstrates a "systematic divergence between the fundamental notions of logical theory and the categories operative in our practical assessment of arguments."[35] The result of Toulmin's analysis is a constructively postmodern account of logic in which "logic is concerned with the soundness of the claims we make—with the solidity of the grounds we produce to support them, the firmness of the backing we provide for them . . . with the sort of *case* we present in defense of our claims."[36]

Here the case approach to normative questions can be seen in a more general form. Toulmin writes, "Logic . . . is generalized jurisprudence. Arguments can be compared with law-suits, and the claims we make and argue for in extra-legal contexts with claims made in the courts, while the cases we present in making good each kind of claim can be compared with each other."[37] Finally, Toulmin proposes that the rational process may appropriately be characterized with reference to "the procedures and categories by using which claims-in-general can be argued for and settled."[38]

A MORE GENERAL TREATMENT OF JUDGMENT

Judgment, whether in terms of warranted assertability in Dewey or the convergence of judgmental agreements in Wittgenstein or the jurisprudential rationality of Toulmin, has been repeatedly offered as a central element of a constructively postmodern engagement of uncertainty and indeterminateness. In providing a more general account of this unifying principle an excellent analysis of the concept of "judgment" by Thomas H. Green should prove helpful. Green acknowledges two core uses of the term. Although in the formulations of classical logic judgment is synonymous with assertion, statement, or proposition, it is also used more generally to refer to a distinctive capacity of human beings. The nature of this capacity may be discerned in our the uses of the expressions "a person of sound judgment" or "one of good judgment." Green's analysis of judgment includes therefore both its capacity or activity sense and the assertions or propositions through which the products of this activity are ultimately expressed.

In ordinary experience we use "judging" productively to refer to the following specific kinds of activity or combinations of them: ranking or grading, estimating, and predicting. Although the activities of ranking, estimating, and predicting all involve standards, there is often very active disagreement among people about the relevance and application of such standards. The jurisprudential procedural analyses of Toulmin, however, encourage us to look carefully beyond specific disagreements to identify the infrastructure within which these disagreements are debated. Such attention to the procedures used to support the activities of judging show that there is a wide scope for productive communication and agreement about how specific judgments should be made. Rules of evidence are developed and argued with a view to increasing the level of confidence we may have in the ways in which information is presented in courts to assist judges or jurors in estimating the credibility of assertions of guilt or innocence. In the area of social policy formulation, care is given to the development of procedures by which controversial issues, which often turn on significantly different core value positions, may be reasonably decided. Even in the area of the arts, procedures and practices are pursued that will increase the level of assurance reasonable people may have in the results of international performance competitions in music or juried exhibitions in the visual arts. In each case effort is directed at considering the views of people with special expertise in the areas at issue, developing standards that are seen as comprehensive and fair, and providing structural protection against the influence of prejudice and other irrelevant considerations in the deliberations. Although we might argue quite persuasively that certain sets of standards may be justified with reference to specific theories of value or measurement, we must also acknowledge that such theories are incapable of being articulated with the level of assurance we rightly expect in other less controversial areas. Procedures and practices that are developed as relevant to specific areas of judgment, if tested in the appropriate venues and if open always to the possibility of further refinement and improvement, may be rationally endorsed even though they may sometimes produce judgments with which individual judges, even expert judges, will disagree. It is a perfectly rational, reasonable position for one to endorse the procedures even if one disagrees from time to time with specific products of those procedures.

Returning to Green's account further clarifies the rationality of this position. Although imprecise and impossible to ground in absolute certainty, a judgment, Green shows, is not merely a guess. To the extent that a guess is merely a hunch or is groundless, it is arbitrary and of little consequence epistemologically. As the grounds in support of an assertion increase in substance and style, even if those grounds fall short of being decisive or conclusive, Green argues that we move quite naturally into the area of judgment. The most significant contribution of Green's account is that it places judging across the vast middle territories of a continuum that has guessing at one extreme and knowing at the other. On Green's account judgments "are truth claims made in the absence of conclusive grounds."[39] If postmodern perspectives on certainty, either deconstructive or constructive, are at all compelling and if the pursuit of ultimately conclusive grounds is a vain quest, then Green's account would show us that virtually all epistemologically productive assertions, whether normative or empirical, will fall into the category of judgment. While there may be no guarantees for certainty except for assertions within closed systems, like tautologies, there is also no reason to view these judgments as necessarily arbitrary or capricious.

In *Cosmopolis* Toulmin notes that intellectually, "unreconstructed Modernity had three foundations: certainty, formal rationality, and the desire to start with a clean slate."[40] The present study anticipates that when this process of reconstruction is further advanced, a properly constructive postmodernism will be seen to have the following distinguishing features; it will be seen to:

- embrace the situational, local complexities of particular cases as evidence of the richness of human experience;
- explore the ways in which thinking, feeling, and valuing commingle in the actualities of human experience;
- embody a naturalistic (like that of Dewey) or juris-

prudential (like that of Toulmin) model of rationality instead of a logico-mathematical one;

• hold truth claims and knowledge claims to be provisional rather than invariable;

• pursue relevant warrants in support of knowledge claims rather than ultimately certain grounds;

• seek to find, exploit, and develop further areas for productive agreement in normative and empirical judgments in prudently nonrelativistic ways; and

• deal constructively with conceptual analysis; the operative form of its questions being "What is there for us to mean by X?" rather than "What do we mean by X?"

In a fully articulated conception of constructive postmodernism, therefore, the activities of judging will be of central epistemological importance, applicable to both the normative and the empirical domains. Renewed scope for a nonarbitrary view of value judgments may be anticipated as well as more modest expectations about the truth status of conventional knowledge claims.

NOTES

1. Stephen Toulmin, *Cosmopolis: The Hidden Agenda of Modernity* (Chicago: University of Chicago Press, 1992), p. 201.

2. See, for example, Geoffrey Hartman, *Criticism in the Wilderness* (New Haven: Yale University Press, 1980).

3. Toulmin, *Cosmopolis*, p. 200.

4. Ibid.

5. John Dewey, *The Quest for Certainty: A Study of the Relation of Knowledge and Action* (New York: Capricorn, 1960), p. 244.

6. Ibid.

7. René Descartes, *Discourse on the Method of Rightly Conducting the Reason and Seeking Truth in the Field of Science*, trans. Laurence J. Lafleur (New York: Bobbs-Merrill Company, 1960).

8. Ibid., p. 7.

9. Ibid.

10. Ibid.

11. Ibid., p. 15.

12. John Dewey, *Logic: The Theory of Inquiry* (New York: Holt, Rinehart and Winston, 1938), pp. 104–5.

13. Ibid., p. 66.

14. Ibid., p. 67.

15. John Dewey, *Art as Experience* (New York: G. P. Putnam's Sons, 1980), p. 35.

16. Ibid.

17. Ludwig Wittgenstein, *Philosophical Investigations*, 3rd ed., trans. G.E.M. Anscombe (New York: Macmillan, 1968), p. 21.

18. See Wittgenstein, *Investigations*, p. 16, for a discussion of "pointing."

19. Ibid., p. 132.

20. Allan Janik and Stephen Toulmin, *Wittgenstein's Vienna* (New York: Simon and Schuster, 1973), p. 225.

21. D. W. Hamlyn, "Epistemology and Conceptual Development," in *Cognitive Development and Epistemology*, ed. Theodore Mischel (New York: Academic Press, 1971), p. 7.

22. Ibid.

23. Ibid.

24. Ibid., p. 8.

25. Ibid.

26. Ibid., p. 20.

27. Stephen Toulmin, "The Concept of 'Stages' in Psychological Development," in *Cognitive Development and Epistemology*, ed. Theodore Mischel (New York: Academic Press, 1971), p. 35.

28. Ibid., p. 38.

29. Ibid., p. 36.

30. Ibid., p. 39.

31. Wittgenstein, *Investigations*, p. 32.

32. Ibid.

33. Albert R. Jonsen and Stephen Toulmin, *The Abuse of Casuistry: A History of Moral Reasoning* (Berkeley: University of California Press, 1988), p. 2.

34. Stephen Toulmin, *The Uses of Argument* (London: Cambridge University Press, 1964), p. 4.

35. Ibid., p. 7.

36. Ibid.

37. Ibid.

38. Ibid.

39. Thomas F. Green, *The Activities of Teaching* (New York: McGraw-Hill, 1971), p. 177.

40. Toulmin, *Cosmopolis*, p. 183.

Part II

Toward Renewal

4

Toward Renewal in Literary Studies

Of all the forms of human passion, Yeats cautioned in his prayerful poem for his daughter, an enmity inspired by ideas is especially corrosive. This poet knew something of the deleterious effects of ideological passion and understood too well that the potent combination of culture and politics can often erode the social underpinnings of civility on which meaningful dialogue depend. In recent years one especially pernicious form of intellectual hatred has taken root in university departments of English and the other humanities as attacks by postmodern revisionists on the settled presumptions of literary intellectuals respecting the nature and structure of literary studies have been parried by often hostile and defensive traditionalists. Passionate disagreement, sometimes to the point of physical confrontation, has characterized this debate over the past two decades, and a ready source of rhetorical fuel has been the "canon" of "great books" that has purportedly dominated intellectual life for centuries. Condemned by many postmodern critics as the hegemony of "dead white males," this canon has been robustly defended by some traditional humanists as containing no less than the essential elements of Western civilization. So much energy has gone into this "battle of the books,"[1] as William Casement subtitles a recent study of the fracas, that it would be worth inquiring whether the principles of constructive postmodernism developed in the last chapter might be useful in clarifying some of the issues in this dispute. It will be particularly interesting to see whether the idea of connecting conceptual distinctions to the underlying purposes of an activity, in this case literary study, can assist us in suggesting a possible resolution to the problem.

THE STRUCTURE OF LITERARY STUDIES

In *The Great Canon Controversy*, William Casement attempted to bring a lower tone of voice to the argument and in so doing to find a reasonable pathway through the disputed territory. After summarizing the role that set books and so-called great books have played in ancient, medieval, and modern education and describing their purpose as seeking a comprehensive account of the human condition, he accepted the idea of a canon as fundamentally a good thing, while offering an inclusionary admonition to the canonically inclined that, consistent with the canon's rationale, it must be periodically updated to make sure that it covers newer perspectives. In order to identify potential new canditates for canonical status, the canonist must be prepared to read very widely. This is, of course, a temperate and helpful position, one shared by many open-minded traditional scholars, but it omits to consider some very important questions embedded in this controversy. First, of course, is the question of what precisely is at issue. That some academics and scholars have been using the term "canon" in their argumentative exchanges does not necessarily mean that there is a canon to fight about. Except in a loose and argumentatively unhelpful metaphorical sense no one has yet to point to a genuine canon in this dispute. Except in such a loose sense the concept of canon arises in the domain of Christian precepts and dogmas, of canonical biblical texts and apocryphal ones, of prescribed and proscribed books. No sane humanist (however canonistic in Casement's sense) could ever endorse the false belief that there is a distinct, enumerable group of books that has been formally certified as obligatory reading for any person educated in literature and the humanities. Just because there is much similarity in the reading backgrounds of many humanists does not establish the existence of a genuine canon. Certainly lists of books judged to be of central importance have been proposed from time to time, but no one has ever suggested that the composition of these lists is not open to very active disagreement among experts. Indeed many serious literary scholars and humanists have often scoffed at the very idea of proposing lists of great books or publishing such sets, believing the territory to be too vast, subtle, and complex for anything more significant to be achieved in the undertaking than an expression of personal or institutional style.

If there is no canon, at least in the strictly repressive sense, then what is the controversy about? What are the real issues in this controversy? Is there a constructive meaning for "canon" to be identified? Certainly there have been genuinely expressed concerns about the race and gender of those writers whose works most often appear as required reading in literature and humanities courses, but is any prescribed list of readings for a course necessarily canonical? The answer here must also be negative, except again in the metaphorical use alluded to earlier. A set list represents a judgment of what is important or even essential with respect to a given subject matter. Consequently courses in "Eighteenth-Century English Literature," "Mannerism," "Introduction to Western Philosophy," and so on will have readings assigned for them that are representative of their subject matters. One evaluates the appropriateness of such lists by this criterion. Again, there will be important similarities and interesting dissimilarities in such lists for the same courses even in the same university departments. Whatever conformities exist here are largely unsurprising and in no way provide evidence *in and of themselves* of race or gender bias, however else they may be flawed.

But, and it is a large "but," a constructively postmodern approach to this set of issues might well turn on the question: Are our subject-matter divisions in literature and the humanities appropriately conceived? And even more significantly: Does the traditional way of structuring knowledge in the arts and humanities continue to make good sense? If there is to be a "canon" in even the most metaphorical sense, on what conceptual territory should it be pursued? The history of academic divisions, disciplines, and departments is both curious and *ad hoc*. Since the establishment of formal curricula in the medieval university, institutional subject matter structures, especially in the humanities, have been affected more by exigencies of economics and politics than by principles of epistemological coherence. If these distinctions have little to do with the underlying purposes of literary studies, it is timely to reconsider whether organizing the study of literature predominantly in unilingual terms, for instance, encourages or hinders the grasp of literary, cultural, and aesthetic concepts and values, or whether questions about literature and the other humanities are better approached within genetic, generic, or other more substantive contexts.

The unilingual structure of literary studies was consolidated in the nineteenth century, before the great industrial and postcolonial migrations had created such compelling multicultural linguistic facts in so many previously homogeneous language-cultures. Before the revolution in language studies that Saussure initiated, the preoccupations of nineteenth-century philologists with the history of word use as a key to contemporary linguistic significance placed important emphasis on each modern language's unique literary record, with their literatures studied as part of each language's semantic genesis. What the French, English, and Spanish preserved as literature, for example, shed important light on the nature of modern meanings and grammar. Well before the rise of structuralist and poststructuralist studies, literary critics, working within university departments structured around nineteenth-century concerns, began to concentrate on literature as literature, even as the philological concerns once central to the modern languages were absorbed by new and vital departments of linguistics. Although establishing "definitive" texts, identifying and authenticating apocryphal ones, and filling in gaps in the historical and biographical record of literary figures continued to be important scholarly activities, understanding literature as a unique cultural or artistic achievement became the central concern of many university-based literary scholars. Aesthetic or "new critical" concerns predominated through the 1960s while more political and deconstructive concerns are current today, but there has been a fundamental continuity of purpose nonetheless. Within this continuing contemporary tradition literary texts are seen to function as culturally valued artifacts that inevitably tap fundamental regions of public meaning and personal significance, of ritual, myth, dreams, the fabric of interpersonal and social judgment, of power, status, and cultural commitment. Consequently a prudently open-ended methodology has prevailed in literary studies, with the intellectual tools of the historian, biographer, psychologist, philosopher, and others vitally important in furthering our understanding of literature as a cultural phenomenon.

This open methodological orientation was, and continues to be, mostly tolerant of new alternative approaches, even if there is often disagreement among literary scholars about the value of any given approach to literary study. Indeed, the rapidity with which the newer deconstructive programs initially took root in university departments may be taken as some evidence for the tolerance embedded in this kind of general methodology, although now there is abundant evidence of an increased rigidity among different emphases, theories, and points of view. If more tolerant, eclectic tendencies have been seriously compromised, important and fundamental purposes in literary studies may likewise be compromised. The need for many approaches to texts and the openness of scholars to the potential value of new ones would appear to rest on firm experiential footing in that some texts do seem to demand more of one kind of analysis than another, just as other texts may prove fairly intractable to certain forms of literary scholarship. As such, the analysis of the complex, complementary, and contextually dependent meanings of texts has variously required proficiency in the disciplinary skills of a variety of associated subject matters. Although there is at present significant discord between deconstructive and more traditional approaches, differences between them with respect to how best to make sense of texts and which aspects to consider most intently, there are legitimate places for both traditional and deconstructive literary scholars within a purpose structure articulated in terms of making more and better sense of texts. However keenly the value and meaning of one scholar's way of exploring textual significance might be challenged by another, elucidating the contexts within which texts gain significance may be seen to remain a common pursuit.

If the underlying purpose of literary study is to make sense of texts, however, then some aspects of the present structural arrangements require significant adjustment. Dividing the subject matter by individual languages would seem, for example, more to impede than to facilitate the task of literary scholars. To consider English literature in discretely autonomous terms is effectively to curtail many significant opportunities to make comprehensive sense of its historical and contemporary texts, since English-language texts often participate in complex relationships with texts in other languages. Moreover, languages like English or French have become a means of articulating, exploring, representing, and celebrating the identities and aspirations of hundreds of cultures and distinctive groups in addition to those groups with a direct lineage to the more culturally homogeneous language users of past centuries. Hence, there are now many distinctive social and cultural currents participating in an increasingly complex and challenging scholarly process of textual understanding.

It is difficult to overstate the importance of this development. To view the texts of these newly legitimated groups of language users in terms that descend from a nineteenth-century, culturally homogeneous unilingual taxonomy is problematic in at least two ways. First, the universe of texts studied must be broadened if these distinctive currents are to be identified and their interpenetrations understood. This expansion is not simply driven by open-mindedness and an inclusionary ethic, but is epistemologically essential to the business of making more and better sense of contemporary textual values. Issues of identity and appropriation, of one culture's struggle to create meaningful spaces for its own legitimacy within the same linguistic frameworks originally used to interpret and thereby control it, create a secondary set of theoretical issues and concerns that no systematic effort to make sense of texts can plausibly ignore. The political dimensions of texts are, therefore, receiving original and important attention, and nascent studies in new forms of political philology seek to show how complex issues of race, gender, and class are embodied in once "neutral" sets of adverbs and class nouns.

In addition to textual politics, even more traditional aesthetic concerns need to be reconsidered in terms of these new complexities. The struggle to wrest distinctive and culturally authentic value from originally inhospitable linguistic materials inevitably imbues the literary artifacts so produced with a special force, grace, and poignancy. Sorting out the dynamics of these values and their connections to social and cultural norms has become a dimension of contemporary textual understanding that is, in turn, extending the meanings of literary quality. Far from being aberrations which need to be accommodated within existing epistemological structures, the multifarious realities of contemporary textual study are actually deepening and broadening the activities of textual understanding.

FLEXIBILITY AND COMPARABILITY

Pursuing adequate answers to contemporary questions surrounding the problem of making sense of texts would seem therefore to move the field inexorably and productively toward greater flexibility and comparability in textual scholarship. Such a pursuit also underscores the value of those newer movements in literary study that seek to understand the way texts and discourse function as emblems and records of the genealogy of power. If nineteenth-century unilingual models are unhelpful, perhaps the twentieth-century institutionalization of systematic comparative literary studies in some universities outside one or another of the modern language departments might be a useful structural model for a constructively postmodern approach to these issues. A comparative model might be most appropriate, for it is often the case that a literary topic that arises within the context of one language's literary traditions, moves naturally into other contexts as well.

A fuller treatment of the origins literary modernism in Chapter One, for example, would have demonstrated the value of approaching some questions of literary study from a genetic, comparative framework. Approaching modernism in such a fashion makes plain the huge influence nineteenth-century French verse and prose had upon the origins of modernism in English-language literature. Contrasting, for example, the colloquial, melancholy music of Eliot's *Prufrock and Other Observations* with the poems of Masefield and Housman, their immediate Georgian antecedents, makes Eliot appear shockingly original; but reading him within the context of the late French symbolists shows only that in the teens of the new century Eliot was brilliantly exploiting elements of the style Laforgue had initiated in the 1880s. So vivid is the influence in terms of diction, cadence, and image—central topics covered in this period of literary history—that once pursued to its sources in Baudelaire, the story becomes even more fascinating. Baudelaire's primary influence is not French but the American Edgar Allan Poe, whose poems he translated into French and whose literary theory, as expressed in "The Philosophy of Composition," became a manifesto of the new French poetry and thereby a pillar of modernism in English.

THE CASE OF ERNEST FENOLLOSA

Yet another line of influence may be instructively pursued through the English and American Imagists—H.D., Richard Aldington, F. S. Flint, Amy Lowell and others—through their chief advocate Ezra Pound to Imperial Japan and Old China. The story is vividly instructive of the power of transcultural and transtemporal lines of textual influence and confluence. An American philosophy professor and advocate of Asian art and poetry, Ernest Fenollosa, dies, leaving his widow looking for a place to send her husband's papers. Knowing the value of the manuscripts and translations her husband had produced and noticing a stylistic affinity between very early imagist verse and the character-by-character English transliterations her husband had produced from classic Asian poetry, especially from the eighth-century Chinese master Li Po, Ezra Pound in London is identified as the happy beneficiary. Among these wonderful papers are essays on Japanese and Chinese culture and a work on *The Chinese Written Character as a Medium for Poetry*, whose "presentational" aesthetic has an immediate and dramatic impact on imagism and modernism. Also in the papers are the Chinese transliterations, which when plainly set out in Pound's best modernist style and published as *Cathay* become arguably his finest poetic achievement.

This brief sketch of the sources of literary modernism illustrates the artistic fact of productive intercultural influences. Just as Asian culture has enlivened and enhanced the development of literature in Europe and America, we observe today artistic models that originated in the West taken up by African and Asian artists and moved into new and valuable directions. A postmodern approach to such intercultural borrowings, such as Edward Said's *Orientalism*, rightly demonstrates the possibility of unjustly coercing one culture's achievements into conceptual categories implicitly protective of another culture's hegemony, a situation in which appropriative appreciation may in fact conceal more subtle forms of political domination. A constructively postmodern approach to this question must also be wary and vigilant in this connection, but it is also prepared to view the *respectful* use of another culture's achievements as a potentially enriching source of transcultural value and communication.

On this point the experience of Fenollosa is most instructive, for his commitment to Japanese and Asian culture occurred at a time when Japan was caught full in the surge for modernization. Toward this end large numbers of Westerners were imported to occupy positions of importance in bureaucratic and academic capacities. In this zeal to modernize, however, Japan's vast cultural riches were devalued, insofar as they represented impediments to progress. Factions of zealous modernizers routinely looted works of art, only to burn them as retrograde rubbish. In such a context it was especially fortunate that one of the experts imported was Ernest Fenollosa, for from the moment of his arrival at the University of Tokyo he became utterly absorbed in, preoccupied with, Asian art and culture. Of this commitment Mrs. Fenollosa wrote, "From the first year he had become deeply interested in an art new to him, the art of Old Japan, and, it must be added, of Old China, too, for in Japan the one cannot be studied without the other."[2] In the literary arts, Fenollosa studied the Noh plays with the actor Umewaka Minoru and Chinese classical poetry with professors Mori and Ariga. Fenollosa's activities, both scholarly and practical, to conserve and restore Japanese art were so extraordinary that the Emperor ultimately made him Imperial Commissioner of Art, in which capacity he served with distinction. After a number of years, when Fenollosa believed the danger to traditional art had been allayed, he felt intuitively that it would be better for the Japanese to assume responsibility for their own arts management and so he made plans for his departure. When Fenollosa left his position, the Emperor presented him with the Order of the Sacred Mirror. Mrs. Fenollosa recalled:

> the court in full regalia, grave Japanese nobles and statesmen standing silently about, all eyes directed on the one foreigner in the great hall, an American, still young, kneeling to receive the highest personal order yet bestowed, and to hear words spoken by the Emperor's own lips, "You have taught my people to know their own art; in going back to your great country, I charge you, teach them also."[3]

Except for a three-year stay in Tokyo from 1897 to 1900, Fenollosa spent the rest of his life studying and lecturing in the United States and England. He died in London in 1910. The Emperor of Japan sent a warship to England to bring his ashes back to Japan, where they were buried with honor in the Temple of Miidera.

At the time of his death, Fenollosa was putting the finishing touches on his massive manuscript "Epochs of Chinese and Japanese Art," which Mrs. Fenollosa was able to prepare for publication in 1912. But Fenollosa had left other incomplete manuscripts with which Mrs. Fenollosa was uncertain what to do: sixteen notebooks containing fragmentary translations of Chinese poetry and Japanese Noh plays and the substance (in very rough form) of an essay on "The Chinese Written Character as a Medium for Poetry." Having seen some of Ezra Pound's verse in one of the little magazines and thinking that Pound's poems instantiated to some degree the principles of poetry that her husband had advocated, Mrs. Fenollosa met with Pound in 1913; he agreed to take charge of the manuscripts and to publish whatever he thought desirable. From the Fenollosa manuscripts, as mediated by Pound, Asian sensibilities entered the mainstream of modernism through *Cathay* (1915), *The Classic Noh Theater of Japan* (1917), and *The Chinese Written Character as a Medium for Poetry* (1918). Of course these sensibilities were changed somewhat in the process of transcultural influence, but the Fenollosa case suggests strongly that not every change need be a corrupting appropriation.

Just as the beginnings of literary modernism are most often approached within the context of English language literature, making fuller sense of modernism moves one naturally into French, American, and Asian texts. Following literary modernism from its first efflorescence in England to its later dominant stylistic position in mid-century thought and culture likewise requires movement between, among, and through the languages of many cultures and nations. The purpose of making sense of English texts can only be accommodated properly, therefore, if the pursuit of pertinent textual relationships moves freely between and among languages. Likewise, making sense of English texts requires attending to the special contexts that distinctive groups of English language users have brought to the domain of English literature. An ideal arrangement would perhaps create new unified departments of comparative textual studies in which the necessary flexibility would be structurally reinforced, but there is no reason that broader acceptance of more flexible and inclusionary practices in textual studies within existing departmental frameworks could not lead similarly, if less directly, to renewal.

WHAT IS THERE FOR US TO MEAN BY TEXTUAL VALUE?

The foregoing discussion has moved freely and silently between two expressions, "literary value" and "textual value." An important contribution of postmodern approaches to texts and discourse, of which the work of Derrida, Foucault, and Paul de Man has been most illustrative, encourages a dismantling of traditional distinctions between imaginative or literary texts on the one hand and more discursive or theoretical texts in the other humanities and sciences on the other. Deconstructive analysis of any text is capable of producing comparably useful discussions of the nature of writing, representation, and the political genealogy of concepts. A constructively postmodern account may, in keeping with the principles articulated in the previous chapter, embrace these possibilities as consistent with the core purposes involved in making sense of texts, but it is also free to consider in positive terms other, more normative possibilities. A key opportunity presented by constructive postmodern thinking is that it may remain intelligible for some literary scholars to speak of literary and other values in connection with texts, even though productive discussions of value cannot establish finally and with certainty that any such claim is ultimately true. A constructively postmodern approach to value, however, is not embarrassed by this admission, since even the most firmly warranted of our scientific beliefs is likewise conditioned by such an awareness.

The proposal here is that a claim about textual value may be most usefully understood as a belief on the part of the person making the claim that the text in question merits serious consideration in respect of its cognitive or aesthetic interest. Simply put, to say that a text has value is to mean that:

(a) the text furthers our understanding of ourselves and our environments whether physical, social, or symbolic. In this case the text is judged to have cognitive quality, or that:

(b) the text possesses interest in the manner and means of its expression. In this case the text is judged to have literary quality, or

(c) both a and b.

It is not essential that the cognitive quality of any text reside within any present, widely accepted disciplinary framework. Works that are judged to present compelling accounts of things no longer believed may have textual value if they are shown to further our understanding of how we have come to develop and manipulate symbolic systems. Alternatively, a claim to cognitive quality may be prompted by a judgment that a given text illustrates a new way of thinking and talking that *might* come to enhance our understanding of ourselves and our environments in the future. Finally, a constructive and distinctly postmodern claim to cognitive quality might involve the principle articulated in the last chapter concerning the complexity and context-dependency of interpersonal meanings and point to the ways in which some traditional literary works offer significant methodological insight into contemporary research questions in the social and behavioral sciences. This particular dimension of the cognitive value of literary texts will be taken up later in much more detail.

LITERARY QUALITY

The idea of literature is inextricably bound to the notion of value. Linguistically it can be argued that the very existence of a concept of "literature" as distinct from the more general notion of writing implies that we wish to hold some specimens of writing up for special attention. As language users we have done so simply to recognize that some forms of writing occasion such heightened responses in so many readers that we seek to objectify this recognition by marking it out with a special concept. Following Dewey, we can say that texts become literary when their symbolic and expressive textures achieve the resolved rhythm of a shaped whole. When a text coheres in this way we value it as an emblem of experiential fulfillment, as an immediate, qualitative display of purposeful integrity. It is crucial to note that the notion of literary quality need not be restricted to those texts conventionally viewed as literary. Consider a text like P. F. Strawson's *The Bounds of Sense*, his famous study of Kant's *Critique of Pure Reason*. On the purely cognitive level Strawson's study explores this most demanding work of abstract philosophy with such sympathy and acute critical awareness that it has been consistently valued by students of Kant and advanced Kant scholars since its publication in 1966. Wholly apart from its philosophical value, however, it possesses, in its lucidity, poise, eloquent directness of expression, and natural prose rhythms, an additional quality that may only properly be called "literary." Like the best exemplars of the functional arts, which achieve aesthetic interest and integrity while superbly accommodating the practical purposes for which they were made, writing of this kind would seem to present significant opportunities for studying the ways in which *what is said is said* may sometimes be independently interesting to readers. Certainly a text need not succeed in its literary possibilities for it to be valued cognitively, but simply because a text is primarily valued for its intellectual contributions does not rule out its potential usefulness in literary study.

To say that the concept of literature marks out aesthetically worthwhile texts does not entail the false belief that all correct users of the concept must agree on which particular texts are worthwhile in this way. The proposed definition of literary quality simply acknowledges that to call a text literary is to commit oneself logically to a judgment that the text possesses value in respect of the manner and means of its expression. All such judgments are, of course, provisional and can be wrong. That judgments are by their very nature provisional and fallible means only that we are routinely compelled in our postmodern uncertainties to formulate views in the absence of conclusive epistemological warrants. It is very important to understand, however, that these constraints are not restricted to the normative domain of literary and other values. Even the firmest empirical beliefs, which have traditionally been considered to have scientifically incontrovertible bases, must now be seen to be judgments—judgments expressed with justifiable confidence, to be sure, but judgments notwithstanding.

Judgments by their nature are things about which people can and will often disagree, but it is crucial to note that this disagreement affirms judgment as a concept, it does not undermine it. We judge in the absence of conclusive evidentiary bases. Some judgments are demonstrably better than others, and history has shown there to be enormous scope for rational dialogue in the absence of certainty. Constructive postmodern interest in those jurisprudential and casuitical models of rationality discussed in the last chapter, as well as contemporary exemplars of such rational processes at work in philosophers such as Ronald Dworkin, point encouragingly toward continuing improvement in our efforts to exploit the scope for rational process among the epistemological uncertainties of our postmodern era. Dworkin's magnificent *Life's Dominion*, published in 1993, is a most persuasive illustration of the scope for appropriately configured rational processes in bringing clarity and constructive support to the thorniest questions of contemporary public policy, namely, euthanasia and abortion.

The definitional possibilities for textual value developed here are offered as potentially useful tools in the renewal of comprehensive and less factious textual studies. They can be useful in this connection, however, only if such possibilities are seen by practitioners in literary studies to enhance the efficacy of their undertakings. Certainly the currents of research and development in most university modern language departments are moving in directions that are consistent with expanding the scope of literary studies into other textual territories, but there is still resistance to these currents by some more traditionally oriented scholars. These scholars are justifiably concerned that such developments may undermine the legitimacy of their preferred modes of inquiry. This need not be the case, however, if textual value is understood, as has been proposed here, to embrace aesthetic concerns as well as the newer expanded interest in more culturally complex cognitive issues. In this way textual value may be taken as the common object of both traditional and newer approaches. Just as existing university departments of English, French, and the like would be wise to encourage more multilingual and multicultural lines of textual inquiry, such departments would also be wise to encourage widening the scope of texts to be approached beyond those traditionally viewed as "literary."

COGNITIVE QUALITY

Inasmuch as a text like Strawson's *Bounds of Sense* may be seen to possess literary as well as cognitive value, it is also the case that some traditional literary texts may be approached more directly as sources of cognitive value. Traditionally studies of "ideas in literature" have focused on the intellectual interest aroused by the notion of time in Proust, for example, or of personal identity in Shakespeare. Such studies have been valuable in showing how verbal artists may also make specifically intellectual contributions that are significant also in nonliterary contexts. Here too the principles of constructive postmodernism may be useful in pointing to potentially *unique* sets of contributions to the understanding, which may flow directly from the nature of the literary intelligence at work in certain kinds of narrative writing. In the previous chapter the problem of reconfiguring rationality in less formal, but more comprehensive terms was seen as inevitable if we wished to pursue cumulative and systematic understanding. It was also seen that meaning and social understanding were so complex and context-dependent that in Toulmin's terms, we needed to return again and again to the minutely observed world of the *particular*, if we wished to gain purchase on these topics.

The growing awareness of the importance of richly observed contexts in coming to terms with problems in the social and behavioral sciences has produced a major postmodern realignment in the nature of sociological and psychological inquiry, away from reductionist quantitative study and toward a more relaxed and sensitively descriptive mode. In the lean and elegant explanatory frameworks of behaviorist psychology, in which the theoretical structures built by J. B. Watson and B. F. Skinner are so similar to architectural ones designed by Mies van der Rohe, explaining and predicting the whole of human experience had been held to be reducible to specifiable patterns of stimulus and response. This psychological correlate of the philosophically modernist "logical atomism" discussed in Chapter One also corresponds to the sociological reductionism of Talcott Parsons, whose pristine theoretical architectonics rested so securely for a time on the naively unproblematic validating principle of "functionality." Postmodern awareness of the limitations of such reductionist representations of meaning and social reality has resulted in the rapid development of what are called "qualitative" research methodologies. Here the detailed study of people engaged in actual practices, naturalistically observed by sociologists or psychologists who may themselves participate in the activities under study, is reported in an openly narrative style. Hoping to capture nuances of meaning and significance in this way, figurative as well as plainly descriptive language has come to be quite widely used. In fact a recent work on qualitative methodology by Alan Peshkin and Elliot Eisner[4] anticipates empirical doctoral dissertations actually written, submitted, and accepted by examiners, *as novels*. Opening social and psychological understanding to literary sensibilities represents, of course, a fairly dramatic rejection of modernist ideals in psychology and sociology.

For scholars in literary studies these developments may suggest several interesting possibilities. What precisely does the achievement of a writer like Henry James represent, if not pointedly detailed observations of densely complex social and interpersonal relations, mediated by a painfully acute and sophisticated sensibility and imaginatively represented as works of fiction? Is Henry James to be studied as a social scientist as well a literary artist? Are *all* novels comparably significant in terms of this sort of cognitive value? Is the key to this sort of value the novel as such or the particular sorts of intelligence at work in particular novelists? Is the basic repertoire of intellectual skills used in qualitative scientific research essentially literary? To what extent can certain literary artists' skill at inferring dependable generalizations respecting patterns of social meaning, behavior, and interpersonal judgment be documented and analyzed? In short: Do some literary artists have a special value to offer to social scientists as they seek to understand and realize their own methodological ambitions?

These questions are at the core of the next two chapters. It will be argued in Chapter Five that in addition to the exemplary literary value possessed by a novel like Jane Austen's *Mansfield Park*, a work of this kind may also embody independently significant contributions to epistemology, semiotics, and methodological theory in the social and behavioral sciences. Likewise, in Chapter Six, the work of Henry James and others will be shown to contain empirically usable data on the nature of the emotions.

NOTES

1. William Casement, *The Great Canon Controversy: The Battle of the Books in Higher Education* (New Brunswick: Transaction Publishers, 1966).

2. Mary Fenollosa, preface to *Epochs of Chinese and Japanese Art*, by Ernest Fenollosa (New York: Dover Books, 1963), p. xiv.

3. Ibid., p. xviii.

4. See Alan Peshkin and Elliot Eisner, *Qualitative Inquiry in Education: The Continuing Debate* (New York: Teachers College Press, 1990).

5

Social Intelligence in Fiction

Seventy years old and gravely ill with the disease that would soon end his life, Lionel Trilling strove to complete a promised address for the 1975 Jane Austen Bicentennial Conference at the University of Alberta. Trilling was too ill to attend the conference and the unfinished paper, "Why We Read Jane Austen," was published the following year in the *Times Literary Supplement*. The paper was prompted by a quite remarkable course on the novels of Jane Austen that Trilling offered at Columbia University in 1973. Intending to lead a class for approximately twenty-five students in which discussion, rather than lectures, would predominate, Trilling was astounded when 150 enthusiastic students presented themselves for the first class meeting. The almost frenzied moral fervor that characterized the desire of these students to continue in the course when their professor told them he could only cope with forty left Trilling with the kind of puzzle he very much enjoyed. Why should Jane Austen, the "presiding genius of measure, decorum, and irony"[1] exercise such attraction for a generation not known especially for its devotion to these qualities?

Like much of Trilling's literary criticism, this essay is an attempt to understand the particularities of his own cultural environment, viewing texts as artful provocations that could bring the political and psychological interiors of educated persons, ever the group of interest to Trilling, more clearly into relief. Here the novels of Jane Austen become a spur to recognizing just how, as educated people, "we have built into the structure of our thought about society the concept of *Gemeinshaft* in its standing criticism of *Gesellshaft*."[2]

Trilling's students, he observed, whose communal impulses arose in opposition to the settled interests embedded in their social structure, were intent to find in the precise and scrupulously observed world of Jane Austen the means of transcending their variously problematic contemporary existence. They could in reading backward vicariously participate in a secondary world in which things presented themselves in far more manageable proportions: a world always attractively described in which visually vivid and compelling natural vistas and minutely detailed commonplaces of daily life provided pleasant backgrounds for stories of interest and significance. In resonating sympathetically with characters arising in a context so agreeably different from their own and in seeing relevance to their own predicaments in the moral lives of such characters, Trilling believed, the students were acting on a fundamental tenet of humanism: that in the paradigms of a past culture our own moral lives may be subjected to rational scrutiny and thereby tested. Here, in the midst of another time's richly observed *Gesellshaft* were ample opportunities for extending and validating the students' own *Gemeinshaft*.

In this way the initial puzzle over the appeal Jane Austen had for these students was resolved by Trilling even as he conducted the interviews necessary to pare his class down to size. As the course unfolded, however, an even more interesting problem began to emerge: Did not the significance of a character's moral circumstances often depend on reference to codes of conduct and manners that while carefully observed by Austen, often lay beside the point of contemporary experience? In discussing the novels with his students Trilling realized that relating the lives of contemporary readers to temporally distant characters presented existential gulfs that only careful attention to the cultural contexts embedded in the novels could bridge. Trilling began to expose and explore these gulfs with his students, and by the end of the course he felt he had virtually undermined the basic assumption of literary education that he and his students had shared at the outset. Trilling notices with some irony that "so far from wishing to bring about the realization of how similar to ourselves are the persons of a past society, it was actually the dissimilarity between them and us that I pressed upon."[3] Inevitably such a pedagogical stance would cast "doubt upon the procedure by which humanism puts literature at the service of our moral lives."[4]

After the course ended, Trilling's continuing preoccupation with this problem led him to the work of Clifford Geertz, whose paper "From the Native's Point of View: On the Nature of Anthropological Understanding" provided a perspective within anthropological theory for Trilling's further reflections. Geertz argued in this paper that empathetic connections (the sort of connective rapport that Trilling believed the basic assumption of literary education to rest upon) between the anthropologist and the members of another culture are of little consequence in the process of making sense of that culture. Far more important is "searching out and analyzing . . . words, images, institutions, behaviors—in terms of which . . . people actually represent themselves to themselves and to one another."[5] Trilling concludes that the importance and complexity of this process, known in social science methodology as "ethnography," substantially confounds the humanist's "rather simple view of the relation in which our moral lives stand to other cultures"[6] and that a crucial perspective on the imaginative experience of the past is a reconstruction of the cultural context in which the experience arose.

Trilling brings us therefore to see the importance of ethnographic skills and perspectives in understanding Jane Austen's novels. It may be productive now to ask what role, if any, this same set of skills and perspectives can play in understanding the essence of her craft. Here again it will be helpful to turn to Clifford Geertz.

THICK DESCRIPTION

For Geertz the animating principle of ethnography is not to be found in methodological textbooks that provide detailed instruction in how to establish rapport, choose informants, keep notes, develop genealogies, and so forth. Such methods are useful only insofar as the person intending to develop knowledge and understanding of another culture also possesses the ability to interpret the significance of words and behaviors within the contexts of the group being studied. To represent this ability Geertz borrows a notion from the philosopher Gilbert Ryle, whose own work on human action and the concept of mind had led him to formulate the idea, since Geertz so widely used in the social and behavioral sciences, of *thick description*.[7]

In a pair of essays Ryle shows that the meaning of a gesture like the contracting of one eyelid cannot be established by such a "thin" description; rather, its significance depends on the way the gesture is used within a context. Insightful exploration of the relevant context will provide us, for example, with a means of seeing the "immense but unphotographable difference between a twitch and a wink."[8] That eyelid's contraction *might* be a simple reflexive twitch, if in context there is no reason to believe it is serving any other purpose. Or if it is pointedly done according to an already understood code, it could be a invitation to another person or persons to participate in a private understanding or joke. But Ryle does not stop with this conspiratorial possibility, much to Geertz's satisfaction; he gives examples of how a wink might signify among a group of boys, effectively opening a "Chinese box" of possible actions this behavior might imply. In adition to one boy's simple wink, another boy, "perhaps . . . new to the art . . . winks rather slowly, contortedly and conspicuously. A third boy, to give malicious amusement to his cronies, parodies this clumsy wink."[9] To this can be added yet another boy, "trying by private rehearsals to prepare himself effectively to parody a wink."[10] Making sense of an eyelid's contraction, therefore, requires a thick description steeped in inferences about intentions, purposes, and codes of social meaning.

Geertz was right to be excited by this notion, for the kind of description aimed at in anthropological understanding must be very, very thick with possibilities for significance and meaning. Geertz is also right to realize that in describing, the ethnographer is always interpreting, always applying patterns of human interaction to specific events, and always aiming to develop interpretive structures of greater explanatory force. Interpretation and explication are the means of thick description, and their productive use is the central tool in ethnography. A related use of thick description can be found in the field of ethnomethodology, a distinctly sociological form of ethnography in which there is often much closer cultural affinity between the researcher and the group being studied. Intent on using sociological knowledge to improve the plight of the late nineteenth-century underclass, a group of sociologists at the University of Chicago, led by George Herbert Mead and Charles Horton Cooley, developed a new form of "scientific" sociology. The Chicago School, as it was called, rejected the behavioristic models then prevalent in favor of studying such social-psychological phenomena as consciousness, action, and interaction. Notwithstanding much success, the Chicago School's emphasis on suitably thick descriptions of research subjects' personal orientations to their situations became less popular among sociologists as more neutral descriptions of structure and statistical analyses of more impersonal variables became the hallmarks of sociology in the midcentury. But the ideas developed by Mead and others did not die out. Erving Goffman, a key figure in the development of contemporary ethnomethodology, began his own work with a careful study of the Chicago School. His dramaturgical analysis is a variant of the kind of symbolic interactionism practiced by Mead and his followers. Goffman's analysis "concentrates on the form of interaction itself rather than the structures it creates, sustains or changes"[11] and stresses a fundamental affinity between theatrical performance and our daily forms of social interaction. The theory of consciousness and action embedded in Alfred Schutz's *The Phenomenology of the Social World* (1932) is a clear influence on the work of his student and the chief theorist of ethnomethodology, Harold Garfinkel, whose *Studies in Ethnomethodology* established ethnometholodogy as a distinctive sociological perspective. Here thick description aims at understanding the methods people use to make sense of their own experience of the world or, more strongly and echoing Schutz, how people use language socially to construct their reality.[12] Thick description, therefore, is a tool in understanding other people, whether the groups to which they belong are in a wholly different culture or are part of one's own social structure.

If, as Geertz maintains, thick description is not captured in the methodological analyses of ethnography, we may ask, "Why?" One excellent possibility is that in its subtle blend of imagination, inference, and attention to the materials of social interaction it is more art than craft, and as such liable to exist in many unlikely places. Certainly historical antecedents have been identified in the literature on ethnology, practitioners of ethnography who wrote before the advent of modern cultural anthropology. Nigel Fielding astutely notes that Thucydides's *History of the Peloponnesian War* was not only a historical narrative but a work that "shed a most vivid light on the workings of the Greek political mind, on the motives of the actors and the arguments which they used."[13] In the work of this ancient historian the contemporary ethnographer's need to document events within the contexts of meaning and significance of the people participating in them finds a sympathetic precursor. Later, Fielding notes, these concerns would be separated out from the field of historiography "and become a distinct method for the study of unfamiliar cultures."[14]

Colonial expansion in the nineteenth century, especially within the British Empire, produced another unlikely spur to the development of the art of thick description. Insightful letters home from colonial administrators and their abundant support personnel began indirectly to provide information useful to the task of coordinating centrally the geographically and culturally diverse colonial territories. Examination of surviving specimens shows that many letter writers became careful students of local practices and developed insights into "native" ways of thinking and perceiving. Such epistolary achievements in fact spurred the development of early anthropology. As district commissioners, those custodians of British interest who represented the Crown in local settings, came to be required to send detailed reports home describing the social and cultural systems of their jurisdictions, it was noted that not every report conveyed the same quality of information. Depending on the observer's acuity of perception and the observer's fluency in articulating those perceptions, the usefulness of such reports could vary widely. Based upon the best of these accounts early anthropologists developed a detailed protocol, a generic "notes and queries" approach that could be taken by any administrator (however acute, or not) to any local informant in any part of the Empire to develop useful information. This protocol, which attempted to make explicit the observational skills embedded in the successful reports home, can, without too much strain, be seen as a very early attempt to understand the nature of the art of thick description. The notes and queries protocol was a very successful, if now somewhat quaint, variety of armchair anthropology in which the social scientist could develop data, as it were, by remote control.

John Donne observed centuries ago that letters, sympathetically composed, can mingle souls. The art of closely observing environments whether natural, social or symbolic and finding ways in language to communicate those observations is of central importance to the novelist as well as the letter writer. Just as letters have been shown to be significant, if incipient, sources of thick description, the balance of this chapter will emphasize another important line of relevance to the development of contemporary ethnography, that of the novelist. In so doing, the discussion will provide an opportunity to explore the cognitive value of a group of texts normally considered predominantly in terms of their literary quality. In the context of this study as a whole, this kind of treatment will further test the constructively postmodern notion, developed in the last chapter, that some novelists may have independently significant contributions to make to the theoretical problem of representing interpersonal meaning and judgment in the social and behavioral sciences. In addition to Jane Austen, whose subtle delimitation of manners and norms among the provincial middle classes of Regency England provide so accurate an account of its moral compass, the work of two other English novelists, Barbara Pym and Anita Brookner, will provide further illustrations of how theoretically pertinent knowledge may be found embedded in some literary texts. A careful reading of *Mansfield Park*, *A Glass of Blessings*, and *Hotel du Lac* will show that this dimension of imaginative accounts is grounded in the skill that some literary artists have for inferring dependable generalizations respecting patterns of social meaning, behavior, and interpersonal judgment. It will also strongly suggest that the basic repertoire of intellectual skills used in ethnography is essentially literary.

JANE AUSTEN

For a single woman without a private income, the precincts of the social world Jane Austen observed so finely in her novels were largely determined by her parents' choices. Brief educational sojourns at Southampton and Reading aside, Jane was "never to live anywhere beyond the bounds of her immediate family environment,"[15] and had she lived longer than her forty-two years and remained unmarried she would have had similarly to defer to her brothers in virtually all matters financial and social. Notwithstanding these constraints, as the youngest daughter (among eight children) of a Tory parson, she had throughout her life a busy social and an extended family life on which to draw for her work. While such insularity might have been a handicap for a writer otherwise gifted, it provided Jane Austen with abundant opportunities for studying closely the manners and mores of her own social group. Since this group was one in which the laws of primogeniture and inheritance, the acquisition of incomes and "livings," and the pursuit of advantageous marriages were of central concern to the gentry and professional classes, the subtle ways in which these factors permeate the social fabric and influence the sphere of moral judgment became the object of her "ethnographic" focus and the subject matter of her artistic substance.

The distinction just offered between subject and substance is meant to underscore F. R. Leavis's view in *The Great Tradition* that Jane Austen does not "offer an 'aesthetic' value that is separable from moral significance."[16] Her insights into the moral lives of her acquaintances are simply consolidated artistically in the creation of her literary characters and never contrived in a way that places "her interest in 'composition' . . . over against her interest in life."[17] Indeed, Leavis sees Jane Austen's solution of aesthetic problems of organization and development in her art as part of her larger and more significant "preoccupation" with understanding the moral environments of her circle. "She is intelligent and serious enough to be able to impersonalize moral tensions as she strives, in her art, to become more fully conscious of them and to learn what, in the interests of life, she ought to do with them."[18] Leavis acknowledges Austen to be the first novelist to represent the specifically modern personality and the culture in which it arose.

Concerned ostensibly with the trivial daily comedy of small provincial family life, the ironical exploration of emotion and conduct, Austen's subject matter alters very little through her work. She said that "three or four families in a Country Village is the very thing to work on" and referred to the object of her study as "the little bit (two inches wide) of ivory on which I work with so fine a brush."[19] Such "self-imposed standards of meticulous accuracy"[20] coupled with the astuteness of her scrupulous observational skills would be among the most desirable achievements for any contemporary ethnographer.

It has been often said that Jane Austen's novels are all grounded in the same subject matter: courtship and marriage. The details of Austen's personal situation already presented would explain why a young woman of profound intelligence would find the study of such a subject of such interest and significance, and why there would be so many opportunities for pertinent observation, examination, and analysis in the domestic careers of her female relations and acquaintances. In *Mansfield Park* especially there is abundant evidence of the intellectual products of Jane Austen's social studies. The opening passage in setting the context of the novel is also a minute treatise on the ingredients of the advantageous conjugal contract:

> About thirty years ago, Miss Maria Ward of Huntingdon, with only seven thousand pounds, had the good luck to

captivate Sir Thomas Bertram, of Mansfield Park, in the county of Northampton, and to be thereby raised to the rank of a baronet's lady, with all the comforts and consequences of an handsome house and large income. All Huntingdon exclaimed on the greatness of the match, and her uncle, the lawyer, himself, allowed her to be at least three thousand pounds short of any equitable claim to it. She had two sisters to be benefited by her elevation; and such of their acquaintance as thought Miss Ward and Miss Frances quite as handsome as Miss Maria, did not scruple to predict their marrying with almost equal advantage. But there certainly are not so many men of large fortune in the world, as there are pretty women to deserve them. Miss Ward, at the end of half a dozen years, found herself obliged to be attached to the Rev. Mr. Norris, a friend of her brother-in-law, with scarcely any private fortune, and Miss Frances fared yet worse. Miss Ward's match, indeed, when it came to the point, was not contemptible, Sir Thomas being happily able to give his friend an income in the living of Mansfield, and Mr. and Mrs. Norris began their career of conjugal felicity with very little less than a thousand a year. But Miss Frances married, in the common phrase, to disoblige her family, and by fixing on a Lieutenant of Marines, without education, fortune, or connections, did it very thoroughly. She could hardly have made a more untoward choice.[21]

Family, fortune, income, education (which, for a lady, would include "accomplishments" like drawing, singing, playing, sewing, etc.), and connections form one set of variables to be explored in pursuing or assessing a match; while character, social grace, and appearance (down to the specific values to be placed on individual facial and bodily features!) provide still further criteria. Mary Crawford observes in the novel that she "would have every body marry if they can do it properly; I do not like to have people throw themselves away; but every body should marry as soon as they can do it to advantage."[22] Doing so competently, Jane Austen shows, can be a complex and difficult undertaking, particularly as the just application of these standards may at any time be effectively undermined by the disrupting influences of intemperate passion. The Romantic

indulgence of passion, while fit perhaps for the grotesque amuse-
ments of *Northanger Abbey*, is simply beside the point of responsible
social life in Jane Austen's milieu.

In such an environment, a gentleman's ability to read smoothly
the behavioral signals that indicate a young woman's status in the
social rituals of courtship becomes quite important. On Jane Austen's
account of the norms at work in these matters, a young woman only
begins to have a social identity independent of the domestic setting
(in which she may be "noticed" by family and friends of the family)
when she is "out." To be out in Jane Austen's set means to be out of
the home and eligible for appropriate social relationships. In
Mansfield Park, Mary Crawford presents the results of Austen's study
of the socially eligible young lady in a spirited conversation about
Fanny Price with the brothers Bertram:

> "I begin to understand you all, except Miss Price," said
> Miss Crawford, as she was walking with the Mr. Bertrams.
> "Pray, is she out, or is she not?—I am puzzled.—She dined
> at the parsonage, with the rest of you, which seemed like
> being *out*; and yet she says so little, that I can hardly sup-
> pose she *is*."
>   Edmund, to whom this was chiefly addressed, replied,
> "I believe I know what you mean—but I will not under-
> take to answer the question. My cousin is grown up. She
> has the age and sense of a woman, but the outs and not
> outs are beyond me."[23]

It should be acknowledged here that in terms of the story of *Mansfield
Park*, Fanny is admittedly a difficult case for the acute Miss Crawford
to comprehend. As Edmund says, she is grown and (astonishingly)
sensible, but yet her behavior is ambiguous. This ambiguity in
Fanny's role derives from the circumstances of her attachment to
the Bertram family. Fanny is the eldest daughter of the poorly married Frances, and Mrs. Norris, determined to assist one sister at the
expense of another:

> could not get her poor sister and her family out of her
> head, and that much as they had all done for her, she
> seemed to be wanting to do more; and at length she could

not but own it to be her wish, that poor Mrs. Price should
be relieved from the charge and expense of one child entirely out of her great number. [24]

That child Fanny, at the age of nine, came to live at Mansfield Park
under the sponsorship of her aunts to be raised "among" them. It is
Sir Thomas Bertram, once he is fixed with the actual custodial obli-
gations descending from Mrs. Norris's generous act, who is careful
to enlist Mrs. Norris in the creation of so subtly correct a role for
Fanny in the home of her cousins that it can confound even the percipient Miss Crawford:

> "There will be some difficulty in our way, Mrs Norris,"
> observed Sir Thomas, "as the distinction proper to be made
> between the girls as they grow up; how to preserve in the
> minds of my daughters the consciousness of what they
> are, without making them think too lowly of their cousin;
> and how, without depressing her spirits too far, to make
> her remember that she is not a *Miss Bertram.* I should wish
> to see them very good friends, and would, on no account,
> authorize my girls the smallest degree of arrogance to-
> wards their relation; but still they cannot be equals. Their
> rank, fortune, rights, and expectations will always be dif-
> ferent. It is a point of great delicacy, and you must assist
> us in our endeavors to choose exactly the right line of con-
> duct."[25]

Mrs. Norris obliges, carefully creating subtle differences in the experience of the three cousins. Fanny's disinclination to learn music
or drawing is, for example, encouraged by Mrs. Norris as she observes to the two Miss Bertrams, "it is not at all necessary that she
should be as accomplished as you are;—on the contrary, it is much
more desirable that there should be a difference."[26]

Thus it is not surprising that Miss Crawford is uncertain as to
Fanny's precise social state. Returning to her conversation with
Edmund and his brother at the point when Edmund confesses con-
fusion about "the outs and not outs," Mary replies:

> And yet in general, nothing can be more easily ascertained.
> The distinction is so broad. Manners as well as appear-

ance are, generally speaking, so totally different. Till now, I could not have supposed it possible to be mistaken as to a girl's being out or not. A girl not out, has always the same sort of dress; a close bonnet for instance, looks very demure, and never says a word. You may smile—but it is so I assure you—and except that it is sometimes carried a little to far, it is all very proper. Girls should be quiet and modest. The most objectionable part is, that the alteration of manners on being introduced into company is frequently too sudden. They sometimes pass in such very little time from reserve to quite the opposite—to confidence! *That* is the faulty part of the present system. One does not like to see a girl of eighteen or nineteen so immediately up to every thing—and perhaps when one has seen her hardly able to speak the year before.[27]

From an ethnographic point of view there is much to be observed here. It is clear that Miss Crawford is both confident and temperate in her understanding of the rules governing the distinction between being out and not out as she commences to articulate them. She observes rightly that as rules, her principles are presented as dependable generalizations, rather than incontrovertible laws of conduct. She then divides her distinguishing principles into two meaning-bearing systems, appearance and behavior, inasmuch as both the close bonnet and colloquial reticence are instances of social meaning. Jane Austen's noting the significance of the bonnet within the context of social interaction is particularly interesting. It is only relatively recently that with the advance of semiotic analysis we have come to approach systematically the "language" of clothing; yet here we find that study perfectly anticipated. There is significance too in Mary's interjection, "You may smile," when her description of the not out girl's appearance and demure manner must have provoked some mirth in her companions, since, as Harold Garfinkle's "breeching experiments" in ethnomethodology have shown, making an implicit and previously unrecognized meaning explicit is often a cause for laughter.

Even more significant than any of these observations, however, is the epistemological differential established between Miss Crawford's knowledge of this social role and that of Edmund, who said earlier, "I believe I know what you mean—but I will not undertake to answer the question . . . the outs and not outs are beyond me."[28] Here

Edmund acknowledges that he understands the rules in practice even though he is unable to articulate them in principle. This is a very important distinction, both empirically and philosophically. As a socially competent person, Edmund *knows* much more about the rules at work in systems of social meaning that he can *tell*. He knows *how* to behave consistently with the meanings encoded in social interactions even though he might not know *that* specific sets of articulated principles may be used to explain or predict his behavior. Miss Crawford however, like her creator Jane Austen, possesses the intelligence and skill to move beyond simple social competency to social understanding. This move from implicit or tacit knowledge to explicit or propositional knowledge requires both a compelling interest in social meaning and the far more difficult intellectual activity necessary to represent that meaning in publicly accessible form.

A SPECIAL PROFICIENCY

This intellectual skill, of course, turns on the distinction between practice and theory; and as thinkers as diverse as Aristotle, Ryle, Polanyi, and Geertz have shown, proficiency in *doing* does not automatically translate into *understanding.* To understand a social practice requires the application of a theory or often the even more difficult business of generating one. In such a theory sets of concepts (and principles respecting the relationships of those concepts to each other and to actual practices) provide a framework for explaining that practice. Once a practice is successfully explained it is, in terms of the earlier discussion of Geertz, capable of being justly or thickly described. A thick description of a practice makes it understandable, unsurprising, and even predictable. In Miss Crawford's conversation with the brothers Bertram, the practical uses of such theoretical representations are soon pointed out by Tom. Mary observes:

> "It is much worse to have girls *not out*, give themselves the same airs and take the same liberties as if they were, which I *have* seen done. *That* is worse than any thing— quite disgusting!"
>
> "Yes, *that* is very inconvenient indeed," said Mr. Bertram. "It leads one astray; one does not know what to do. The close bonnet and demure air you describe so well (and nothing was ever juster) tell one what is expected; but I

got into a dreadful scrape last year from the want of them. I went down to Ramsgate for a week with a friend last September . . . my friend Sneyd . . . his father and mother and sisters were there, all new to me. When we reached Albion place they were out; we went after them, and found them on the pier. Mrs. and the two Miss Sneyds, with others of their acquaintance. I made my bow in form, myself to one of her daughters, walked by her side all the way home, and made myself as agreeable as I could; the young lady perfectly easy in her manners, and as ready to talk as to listen. I had not a suspicion that I could be doing any thing wrong. They looked just the same; both well dressed, with veils and parasols like other girls; but I afterwards found that I had been giving all my attention to the youngest, who was not *out*, and had most excessively offended the eldest. Miss Augusta ought not to have been noticed for the next six months, and Miss Sneyd, I believe, has never forgiven me."[29]

Just as a contraction of an eyelid may or may not be a wink, in this analysis of the meaning of Miss Augusta's behavior and dress, we return to the essence of Ryle's original account of thick description. The importance of interpreting the social meanings of one essential element of courtship, the timely identification of a potential spouse, is the underlying purpose Jane Austen's empirical investigations must have been prompted to serve. Just as Mary Crawford is quick to detect in the case of Miss Price an anomaly, a ill-fitting piece of a social puzzle she is intent to complete, so too must Jane Austen have improved her understanding of courtship by such continuous detection and analysis. Through her character Mary Crawford in *Mansfield Park*, Jane Austen presents us with a cogent theory of being out and an illustration of a prescient grasp of much contemporary sociology and epistemology—although either lady, real or contrived, might well be perplexed by so ponderous a way of describing such subtle achievements.

In contemporary terms, then, one important element in Jane Austen's art can be described as ethnographic. Her scrupulous attention to the details of social meaning and her ability to notice patterns *and* to make use of them provide object lessons for any student of social meaning. Moreover, her characters' propensity to test these emerging generalizations or rules in still further observations, while detecting and analyzing any discovered anomalies with a view to ever greater representational scope and predictive ability, provides models for any contemporary theoretician of social meaning. Earlier in discussing Clifford Geertz, his disdain for locating the essence of ethnography in formal methodological protocols was duly noted. There Geertz distinguished between the methodological techniques and accepted procedures routinely taught to novice anthropologists and the intellectually more complex and demanding forays into thick description without whose second sight those methodological procedures would be blind. In the account of Jane Austen just presented we have seen some notable evidence for the value one aspect of her art can provide in understanding better the logic of that essential social vision.

SOCIAL INTELLIGENCE

But does the skill so obviously at work in this social vision depend upon a particular intellectual aptitude for its development? Do we see in novelists of manners an especially active form of social intelligence? Certainly people in everyday experience do differ in their ability to act consistently with the rules at work in social settings. At one extreme are the people who often stumble badly in social situations, not knowing just what to say and how to say it, who routinely put their "feet" in their mouths and who commit more than the occasional *faux pas*. Such socially inept people often make other people uncomfortable and uneasy in social situations and are often ridiculed in their absence. At the other extreme are those people who seem always at ease in social situations, no matter how complex and challenging. Such lucky people can sit down to dinner with a group of people of diverse backgrounds and without apparent effort stimulate conversation and good will. In between, with varying degrees of competency, are all the rest of us.

This particular aptitude can in some people's experience rise to a genuine intellectual competence. Certainly Jane Austen shows us that. In fact, Jane Austen's skills in this area meet all the criteria for "an" intelligence outlined by Howard Gardner in his highly influential study *Frames of Mind: The Theory of Multiple Intelligences*. In this work Gardner lobbies for the reconsideration of a multifaceted conceptualization of the notion of intelligence, rather than the formal, univalent models at work in most conventional I. Q. tests.

Gardner's view is that for an intellectual competence to be considered an intelligence, it:

> must entail a set of skills of problem solving—enabling the individual to *resolve genuine problems or difficulties* that he or she encounters and, when appropriate, to create an effective product—and must also entail the potential for *finding or creating problems*—hereby laying the groundwork for the acquisition of new knowledge. [30]

In this way Gardner isolates seven forms of intelligence: linguistic, musical, logical-mathematical, spatial, bodily-kinesthetic, intrapersonal, and interpersonal intelligence. Gardner's discussion of the last two forms is presented in a single chapter called "The Personal Intelligences," and in it both the individual's "capacity" to "access . . . one's own feeling life" (intrapersonal) and "the ability to notice and make distinctions among other individuals" (interpersonal) are discussed at length.[31] Much of his account of interpersonal intelligence is consistent with the views on social meaning already presented here, although his characterization is more concerned with understanding other persons as individuals than it is with understanding social rules. As Gardner asserts, "examined in its most elementary form, the interpersonal intelligence entails the capacity of the young child to discriminate among the individuals around him and to detect their various moods."[32] But Gardner introduces another element that seems to bring it into more proximate analytical territory, for in an advanced form, "interpersonal knowledge permits a skilled adult to read the intentions and desires— even when these have been hidden—of many other individuals and, potentially, to act upon this knowledge—for example, by influencing a group of disparate individuals to behave along desired lines."[33] Gardner's leap from "capacity" to "knowledge," however, obscures precisely that form of *social* intelligence so nicely illustrated by Jane Austen's conversation on being "out" in *Mansfield Park*. There are two kinds of intellectual ability here, and they are quite different, as different as the peculiar casts of mind of Miss Crawford and Edmund Bertram. Edmund's ability to infer codes of social meaning is tacit, therefore inert and incapable of manipulation, whereas Mary's is explicit and active. In order to act upon this knowledge, in Gardner's terms, one must first have the capacity to develop that knowledge. Proficiency in reading other people's intentions and desires does not automatically translate into proficiency in "influencing a group of disparate individuals to behave along desired lines." And again, these skills are radically different in kind.

An expert player of billiards may in fact be behaving consistently with the Newtonian principles a physicist might use to explain his successes without being able to, or indeed even interested in, representing his activity in that way. Likewise the expert physicist who is able to understand each and every move the billiards player makes may be completely inept at playing the game himself. Thus it should not surprise us that a master of musical technique like Pablo Casals was not particularly good at articulating the ingredients of his performance knowledge when teaching, while a musician of somewhat more modest performance ability like Nadia Boulanger became a legendary teacher of performers and composers alike just because she could articulate so well the elements of successful practice. Being proficient and representing proficiency, as Jane Austen and others have shown us, are two different kinds of competency.

It is outside the present purpose to critique Howard Gardner's influential book, but it should not be too great a digression to suggest that his account would be much stronger if it did not conflate what are in fact several structurally distinct intellectual competencies or "intelligences" in his notion of interpersonal intelligence, particularly as he seems to be aware of some of the relevant distinctions. Reading other people's feelings is different from reading a group's implicit rules, and in both instances *understanding* what is read is different still.

BARBARA PYM

Like Jane Austen, Barbara Pym was a close observer and recorder of human social activity; and like Austen, Pym was aware that the locus of social meaning is best understood within the contexts of specific groups and classes. But unlike Jane Austen, whose ethnographic methods must mostly be inferred from her works, Barbara Pym's interest *in* anthropological methodology provides us with still further insight into the nature of social intelligence in the art of fiction. For Barbara Pym the communities of interest and study are centered in the English upper middle classes: the world of the senior civil service, the professions, and the Church. Steeped in the Anglo-Catholic culture of her parents, Pym's stories are taken directly from her life as she lived it, from the comfortable and happy

home in Shropshire where she lived with cheerful and loving parents and a younger sister to her final years in London. It was as a
student at St. Hilda's College, Oxford, in the early 1930s that Pym
began to display the interest in recording the subtleties of social
behavior that distinguish both her novels and the particular form of
social intelligence under consideration here. As an undergraduate
with an energetic romantic imagination she often would fall in love
with men she did not know, and upon forming such attachments on
sight, she would often follow them or "sleuth,"[34] quietly and unob-
trusively haunting the places they frequented. Significantly, she
would painstakingly make a written record of every detail of such
sightings and observational forays.

Returning to Oswestry in Shropshire after finishing at Oxford,
Barbara Pym began to transform these actual observational notes
into works of fiction. In her first novel, *Some Tame Gazelle*, an actual
ex-lover appears reconstituted in the selfish and arrogant Archbishop
Hoccleve, who, his insensitivity aside, is nonetheless much adored.
This novel, set in the rural England of the 1930s, was reworked and
rewritten several times before its publication in 1950. During the
war Pym's closely recorded observations continued as she detailed
the ways in which life in Oswestry began to change after September
1939. Into a social environment of stability and settled values came
many startling, immediate changes like the blackouts and evacua-
tions. But even more important were the intimations of the subtle
and deeper changes in social attitudes and roles that the war would
usher in. In her major works, the locus of these changes would be
the developing compass Pym used in her lucid explorations of social interactions. There was much to explore: Young women, drawn
into the war effort as nurses or Wrens, had opportunities for experience and achievement independent of the men who, in prewar years,
had almost exclusively defined their social options; new groups of
younger people, spurred on by postwar economic growth, began to
emerge as social beings demanding more than marginal notice in
the world of the moneyed classes; and perhaps subtler still would
be the explorations of those changes in the national consciousness,
as the inevitable smugness of victory and triumph gave way to ambivalence and wariness.

The stressful renegotiation of social roles and expectations among
working-class men and women of all classes produces in postwar
England a kind of golden age of cultural achievement. In literature,
theater, and film, especially, the Age of Anxiety turns a time of awk-

ward social change into an art of vitality, intelligence, and moral force. It may seem odd to locate Barbara Pym's genteel comedies of manners in the same literary territory as the work of Alan Sillitoe, Kingsley Amis, and John Osborne. But it is in the works of Pym that the same painful process of reconfiguring social value undertaken by these "angry young men" is analyzed with such irony and tact.

Ostensibly *A Glass of Blessings* (1958) is concerned with the struggle of Wilmet Forsyth, the chronically underutilized wife of an affluent civil servant, to find open spaces for creativity, intelligence, feeling, and humor within the fairly rigid constraints of a narrowly circumscribed sets of social values and relations. But throughout this novel the stresses just described are powerfully at work beneath the comedy. Although her life now is largely bounded by the social circle of her nearby Anglo-Catholic church, wartime service with the Wrens in Italy had provided Wilmet with opportunities for independence, achievement, and romance. In Italy she met her husband, Rodney, and her now intimate friend Rowena.

Whatever overt changes Wilmet may have exhibited, her narrator's voice in the novel shows that the experience in Italy had created in her a level of expectation for significance that her present life made difficult to achieve. She and Rodney live comfortably, yet uneasily, in the home of his mother, Sybil, a strong-willed, independent, and competent woman thriving on the dustier fringes of academe. Deeply interested in the significance of behavior and appearance among her friends and acquaintances, Wilmet's preoccupations with fashion, etiquette, and received opinion make her seem snobbish. Keen to codify and to judge, Wilmet nevertheless does so with such insight and penetration that it is seems permissible to suggest that, like Barbara Pym herself, her real interest is in the social distinctions themselves and not in their invidious use. As a woman of keen perceptions and constrained ambition, she cannot be judged too severely for exercising her considerable social intelligence in this way.

Wilmet is careful to identify the rules governing appropriate behavior for her circle, which, given the ambiguities of social norms in transition, becomes an intrinsically interesting problem. When, in pursuit of meaningful occupation, for example, she attends a committee meeting in the London Settlement, located in a formerly fine residential area, in which her mother-in-law is active, she notes the awkwardness in a fellow attendee's announcement that she, Mary Beamish, had arrived on the trolley bus:

"Ah, the *trolley bus!*" Lady Nollard's tone was full of horror and I realized that she had probably never travelled on one. Not that I had myself very much, for I did not tend to visit the parts of London where they operated.[35]

But Wilmet wistfully acknowledges:

I had noticed them sometimes going to places that seemed impossibly remote and even romantically inviting, but I had never been bold enough to risk the almost certain disillusionment waiting at the other end.[36]

Once underway, Wilmet finds most of the substance of the discussion far less compelling than the social significance of its setting. Her eyes evaluate the contrast between the old fittings and carvings in the once elegant room, in what would have been a very elegant address one or two centuries ago, and its present purpose. The contrast is reinforced as Wilmet is reminded of the way in which the bombing has facilitated the transition between the shabby elegance of rooms like the one in the settlement and the new and ugly blocks of flats that were being built here and there amid the ruins. As these acute reflections proceed, the meeting turns its attention to the meals the Settlement provides for the indigent old people in the neighborhood, as the secretary Miss Holmes, prompted by a suggestion by Mary Beamish that more meat be included in the meal planning, justifies a necessary economy: "'Well, we have to give them a fish dinner one day a week,' said Miss Holmes in a harassed tone. 'We can't *afford* meat every day.'"[37]

As with the trolley busses, Lady Nollard has a helpful comment to make here:

"When I was a girl," said Lady Nollard, "there was an excellent cheap and nourishing soup or broth we used to make for the cottagers on the estate. Quite a meal in itself, made of bones of course, and large quantities of *root* vegetables—turnips, swedes, carrots and so on."[38]

Wilmet eyes her mother-in-law, Sybil, who senses that Lady Nollard will inevitably stray into unacceptable verbal territories like the lower classes, working classes, or simply the poor. In order to avert this social pitfall, Sybil strategically brings the discussion to a close:

> "Yes, of course we do give them good soup," said Sybil, "but I'm afraid they'll have to go on having the fish. As Miss Holmes points out, we can't afford to give them a meat dinner every day. And now for the report on the Youth Club. Mr. Sprong?"[39]

Mr. Sprong, a somewhat distempered young man, eagerly produces a report that darkly stresses the emergence of undesirable elements in the Youth Club.

Behind the comedy of Lady Nollard's interjections lies the proprietary interest with which philanthropists had customarily viewed their beneficiaries. Mary Beamish had called for more meat in the meals, putting Miss Holmes on the defensive, and in so doing simply noted that her own old mother seemed to *need* meat for strength and suggested more meat for the Settlement's meals. In seeing the Settlement's beneficiaries in the same terms as her own affluent mother, Mary is treating these people in what was to become the model for the mid-century. The welfare state, while it lasted, presumed the poor to be people who simply lacked money and advantages and acknowledged their right to be supported and given opportunities for improving their circumstances. The view it was replacing, however, of the poor as a needy caste that should be grateful for the charity of others, is also still very much at work in the Settlement's thinking. It certainly is alive in Mr. Sprong and the Youth Club.

The accuracy of Barbara Pym's social perceptions, the "thickness" of her descriptions of social meaning, arises from the same form of social intelligence that distinguished Jane Austen. Like Austen, Pym was a close observer and recorder of human activity. Her biographer Hazel Holt documents the extent to which Pym filled "her notebooks with her thoughts and observations"[40] about how we constitute society in a thorough and organized way, always complementing observation with notations and inferences. Janice Rossen, another Pym scholar, provides accounts of the work that Pym did with the International African Institute that are of particular value for in coming to understand the ways in which Pym's social intelligence expressed itself. Rossen notes that upon demobilization Pym commenced employment as a research assistant at the Institute and edited its newsletter for many years. While she continued her own writing, Pym increasingly found the methods of ethnography consistent with, and pertinent to, her own program as a novelist, and through their conscious use, a means of honing her skills as a social observer:

> the discipline of anthropology itself became increasingly important to Pym as a novelist. She grew to think of herself as employing its research techniques in her fiction. In interviews and talks near the end of her writing career she spoke of engaging in "field work," or of employing an anthropologist's "detachment," or of practicing a sociologist's "technique of observation."[41]

As illustrated in *A Glass of Blessings*, Pym scrutinizes her chosen English community, with candor and astute perception, as if it were a "primitive tribe with strange customs and bizarre rituals."[42] Thus the anthropological strain in Pym's writing bears directly on her portrayal of English culture. Although she writes in the tradition of the realistic novel, she also writes as a social scientist in her meticulous notation of detail and cultural surface. She saw her own method of composing as observing life around her and taking from it the exact events that comprised her fiction.

ANITA BROOKNER

Ryle's work on thick description demonstrates emphatically that phenomena do not speak for themselves. Just as the same behavior can be seen as a wink or a twitch, depending on the concepts we bring to bear on his famous example, so too have Jane Austen and Barbara Pym shown us that the perceptual materials of daily life are infused with significance and meaning for the observer who is socially acute enough to notice and represent those meanings. The particular gallery of social intelligence in fiction assembled here has Anita Brookner as its concluding exhibit. Like Jane Austen, Anita

Brookner's high purpose is to analyze the moral complexities of responsible behavior; but unlike Austen, whose struggle occurred substantially within contexts of normative stability, Brookner's pursuit negotiates far more challenging, indeterminate environments. In Brookner's novels educated, affluent people still resonate within a basic framework of accepted roles and values, what Brookner views as a natural arrangement, but remain ultimately unfulfilled. Blocked by inert temperaments, caught between aspiration and actuality, Brookner's men and women find themselves in stunted and attenuated relationships. Organized around "a compendium of Brookner motifs—the literal or figurative orphan, the solitary and alien heroine, the dualism of observer and participant—all ultimately invested in a characteristically ambivalent critique of Romantic myth,"[43] as John Skinner has aptly commented, the many novels may sometimes appear predictable. But viewed organically, the strikingly displayed resemblances from novel to novel also show subtle variations that only reinforce the interplay between Brookner's moral and aesthetic ambitions. In such a thematically unified series of finely wrought individual novels, the materials of experience, which resist fulfillment in life, are resolved harmoniously as aesthetic elements in art. Brookner writes to structure her own experience, moral and aesthetic. For this reason one can speak of Austen and Brookner in terms of comparably significant achievements.

The central character of *Hotel du Lac*, Edith Hope, is an intelligent, middle-aged writer of romantic fiction whose life has become unbalanced by her relationships with men. Quiet and self-effacing, she finds herself the unlikely protagonist in a piece of high public drama when she chooses not to appear at her own wedding. Having created problems for so many people close to her by her action, she is dispatched by her friend Penelope to Geneva, to a resort hotel out of season, to recover her senses. Edith believes that women prefer to believe the old myths about romance and happiness, and her own hopes in this direction work against the good, practical reasons for seriously considering two marriage proposals, one from the embarrassed Geoffrey Long, whose disappointment at the altar has already been alluded to, and another from Philip Neville, a wealthy businessman also staying at the Hotel du Lac. Neville offers Edith an open marriage of convenience on the most mutually attractive and persuasive terms, with nothing as ephemeral as love or passion to complicate things. Edith considers and resolves to accept each of these proposals in turn, but each connection is ultimately rejected. At the novel's end, Edith returns to London and to an affair with the self-absorbed and happily married man she loves.

The distorting influence of Edith's "hope" wreaks many bits of mischief on her perceptual acuteness. Unlike the socially intelligent characters in Austen and Pym discussed here, Edith is continually making incorrect inferences about the significance of social signs and meanings. It is Brookner's social intelligence that permeates the settings within which Edith's misjudgments, essential to the theme of the novel, occur. The inmates of the hotel are perfectly delineated by Brookner through Edith's gradually corrected and improving perceptions. Mrs. Pusey, for example, is first seen by Edith as a shimmering lady of status and scope, only to be understood ultimately as a much more common specimen of bourgeois affectation. At the other end of the pertinent spectrum, a small, gruff, elderly woman with a countenance not unlike a bulldog, who is initially "read" by Edith as a Belgian confectioner's likely widow, is in actuality a countess. Both the contrived and mannered social grace of Mrs. Pusey and the Comptesse de Bonnueil's disdain for middle-class "etiquette" do not reveal as much social meaning to Edith as they possess expressively in Brookner's portraits. The thematic interest of this novel may be seen to turn, in part, on Brookner's use of social intelligence as a literary device.

It is not the astutely mediated perceptions that Brookner creates for Edith with which the final illustration offered of social intelligence in the art of fiction will be concerned, but with the unmediated narrator's description of the meaning of the Hotel du Lac itself. Brookner details the implicit significance of the appearance and style of the Hotel so deftly that she demonstrates in a single paragraph the fact that buildings, like winks and bonnets, may also be variously and thickly described:

> The Hotel du Lac (Famille Huber) was a stolid and dignified building, a house of repute . . . used to welcoming the prudent, the well-to-do, the retired, the self-effacing, the respected patrons of an earlier era of tourism. It had made little effort to smarten itself up for the passing trade which it had always despised. Its furnishings, although austere, were of excellent quality, its linen spotless, its service impeccable . . . it took a perverse pride in its very absence of attractions, so that any visitor mildly looking for a room

would be puzzled and deflected by the sparseness of the terrace, the muted hush of the lobby, the absence of piped music, public telephones, advertisements for scenic guided tours, or notice boards directing one to the amenities of the town. There was no sauna, no hairdresser, and certainly no glass cases displaying items of jewelry; the bar was small and dark, and its austerity did not encourage people to linger. [44]

The ethnographic aptitude that enables Anita Brookner to present such a subtle and complex descriptive analysis of the Hotel du Lac is animated by a form of intellectual ability here called social intelligence. Together with their companion exhibits, these few examples from Brookner have been used to illustrate how such intelligence permeates one kind of fiction. In offering this account, no claim is made that all successful writers of fiction possess this particular kind of intelligence in degrees comparable to Austen, Pym, or Brookner. Neither has it been suggested that an aptitude for ethnography automatically transfers into a talent for writing fiction. What has been maintained is that there is a natural affinity between the skill of ethnography and the kind of social intelligence that animates thick description, on the one hand, and one important tradition of achievement in the art of the novel, on the other. In this constructively postmodern way, one is justified in valuing novels not only for the ways in which their intrinsic aesthetic materials may be successfully resolved, but also because a novel just may contain important insight into the complex and implicit meanings inherent in its social environments.

NOTES

1. Lionel Trilling, "Why We Read Jane Austen," in *The Times Literary Supplement*, no. 3860 (March 5, 1976), p. 251.

2. Ibid., p. 250.

3. Ibid., p. 251.

4. Ibid.

5. Ibid., p. 252.

6. Ibid.

7. Clifford Geertz discusses thick description in his "Thick Description: Toward an Interpretive Theory of Culture" in *The Interpretation of Cultures* (New York: Basic Books, 1973), pp. 3–30.

8. Gilbert Ryle, "The Thinking of Thoughts," in *Collected Papers* (Lon-

don: Hutchinson & Co., 1971), 2: p. 482.

9. Ibid.

10. Ibid., p. 483.

11. Jonathan H. Turner, *The Structure of Sociological Theory*, 4th ed. (Belmont, Calif.: Wadsworth Publishing Company, 1986), p. 391.

12. Further analysis of the ethnomethodological connection to ethnography may be found in George Ritzer, *Sociological Theory* (New York: Knopf, 1983); Ritzer's account of the Chicago School has been relied upon in this chapter. See also Erving Goffman, *Presentation of Self in Everyday Life* (Garden City, N.Y.: Anchor, 1959); and Harold Garfinkel, *Studies in Ethnomethodology* (Englewood Cliffs, N.J.: Prentice-Hall, 1967).

13. Nigel Fielding, "Ethnography," in *Researching Social Life*, ed. Nigel Gilbert (London: Sage Publications, 1993), p. 154.

14. Ibid., p. 155.

15. William Austen-Leigh and Richard Arthur Austen-Leigh, *Jane Austen: A Family Record* (London: Macmillan, 1989), p. 49.

16. F. R. Leavis, *The Great Tradition* (London: Chatto & Windus, 1948), p. 16.

17. Ibid.

18. Ibid.

19. Austen-Leigh, *Jane Austen*, p. 191.

20. Ibid.

21. Jane Austen, *Mansfield Park* (London: Richard Bentley & Son, 1892), pp. 1–2.

22. Ibid., p. 36.

23. Ibid., p. 41.

24. Ibid., p. 3.

25. Ibid., p. 8.

26. Ibid., p. 15.

27. Ibid., pp. 41–42.

28. Ibid., p. 41.

29. Ibid., p. 43.

30. Howard Gardner, *Frames of Mind: The Theory of Multiple Intelligences* (New York: Basic Books, 1983), pp. 60–61.

31. Ibid., p. 239.

32. Ibid.

33. Ibid.

34. Hazel Holt, *A Lot to Ask: A Life of Barbara Pym* (London: Macmillan, 1990), p. 22.

35. Barbara Pym, *A Glass of Blessings* (Harmondsworth, Middlesex, England: Penguin Books, 1980), pp. 19–20.

36. Ibid., p. 20.

37. Ibid., p. 21.

38. Ibid.

39. Ibid.

40. Holt, *A Lot to Ask*, p. x.

41. Janice Rossen, *The World of Barbara Pym* (London: Macmillan Press Ltd., 1987), p. 103.

42. Ibid., p. 106.

43. John Skinner, *The Fictions of Anita Brookner* (London: Macmillan, 1992), p. 19.

44. Anita Brookner, *Hotel du Lac* (London: Jonathan Cape, 1984), pp. 13–14.

Emotional Intelligence

Coming to learn to use words, T. S. Eliot confessed poetically in *Four Quartets*, is a continual struggle, with every new attempt instigating a unique failure and with the skills involved in precise articulation perpetually resisting the writer's apprehension of what most significantly might be said. For Eliot, this struggle is particularly telling in the affective domain, where the intrinsic complexities of feeling and emotion in natural and continual interaction with cognition present intriguing, if intractable, problems for imaginative expression. Each of the poems in *Four Quartets* ends meditatively on the problems of making and meaning in the art of writing. Eliot chose the second of these poems, "East Coker," as the place to engage the problems of language and feeling. That he chose to treat this topic in "East Coker" may have special significance as this part of the poem is most centrally concerned with origins and continuity. Set in the English village from which Eliot's ancestors had emigrated to the United States, it is the site of the now famous open field in which the shades of ancient dancers at a wedding feast are blended with the distant sounds of pipers and drummers. Here in some of Eliot's most primordial and consciously archetypal verse, the durability of the human species resonates sympathetically and in poignant dignity with deeper, more elemental natural forces. In harmonious concord with the vital rhythms of the living earth, the central *element* of "East Coker," Eliot's intemporal celebrants reach forward from the recesses of the past in verse that places human experience in its most fundamental terms.

A work of such masterful formal and thematic coherence encourages the view that Eliot's choice of "East Coker" was a considered one and that the relationship of meaning and feeling in Eliot's poetry and criticism was for him an especially deeply rooted problem and one of continual, if frustrating, technical importance. Indeed, much earlier in his career an original perspective on the relationship between thought and feeling had provided Eliot with a critical lever against the rhetorical excesses of his most immediate predecessors in English-language poetry. In his 1921 review of Herbert J. C. Grierson's edition of *Metaphysical Lyrics and Poems of the Seventeenth Century*, Eliot had considered the problem of thought and feeling in connection with the change in poetic diction that he discerned arising in the later seventeenth century. In vivid contrast to the potent interplay between the intellect and the emotions that had so distinguished Renaissance and earlier seventeenth-century English literature, in the poetry of the latter part of the century thought and feeling had become bifurcated. In this dissociation of sensibility the willful interpenetration of feeling and thinking had been annulled, chiefly through the influence of Milton and Dryden. Unlike the verse of the metaphysical poets, so named by Dr. Johnson in disapprobation of the brash yoking of discordant ideas and images in the verse of Donne and Cowley, the diction of Milton and Dryden was decorous and intelligent, with poetic technique in the elegant service of more discursive tendencies. The emergence of this new diction also affected the substance of poetry, with ideas and "arguments" presented much more explicitly and with much greater scope provided for prosaic description. The dominance of this new diction may have been inevitable, Eliot admits, given Milton's and Dryden's undeniable mastery of technique, but it also represented a fundamental and regrettable evisceration of the poetic image.

THOUGHT AND FEELING

If Miltonic diction is thus eviscerated, then it should not be surprising that eventually the Romantic reaction against it would, in its more fervid pursuit of feeling and emotional awareness, perpetuate, equally regrettably, the dissociated sensibility from the other side of the breech. For the poetically militant young Eliot, writing in a post-Romantic era, the reintegration of thought and feeling was a matter of high priority, for, as Eliot advises, although Tennyson, Browning, and their more ruminative successors certainly do think,

Eliot insists, "they do not feel their thought as immediately as the odor of a rose. A thought to Donne was an experience, it modified his sensibility."[1] That Eliot saw a positive reunification of sensibility in French symbolist verse, particularly that of Jules Laforgue and Tristan Corbière, and was busily following its stylistic exigencies in his own work at the time of his essay on metaphysical poetry is a part of the history of literary modernism already discussed earlier in this study. Eliot's doctrine of dissociated sensibility enjoyed a level of interest in criticism for many years that surprised the poet. Although it is a view that continues to stimulate excitement from time to time, Eliot himself came to see serious limitations in its explanatory power, and thus we find him still struggling in "East Coker" with the underlying issues. In one way, however, the *insight* at work in this doctrine may simply be more significant than Eliot was then capable of representing theoretically. While Dr. Johnson found the inelegant juxtaposition of incompatible ideas in the metaphysical poets untoward, Eliot rightly saw them as a way to provoke "the sensuous apprehension of thought."[2] He was also right in sensing the connectedness of the Renaissance sensibility, of which the metaphysical poets represented the furthest side, to more viscerally grounded forms of cognition. In an important passage in the essay, Eliot astutely characterizes this late humanist sensibility. It is not enough, as Milton and Dryden sometimes direct, to look into the "heart" and write: "that is not looking deep enough. One must look into the cerebral cortex, the nervous system, and the digestive tracts."[3]

But was this simply a commentary on the ways in which Donne and Marvell experienced thought and expressed ideas poetically, or is there something even more significant at work in this powerful connectedness of thought and feeling? If Eliot is right that ideas so apprehended enliven poetic diction, what is the source of this vitality? Is it also the case that the viscerally realized image can similarly move thoughts into more intellectually productive territory? May the viscera tapped in the literary intelligence extend or even generate ideas?

The key to answering these questions is embedded in Dr. Johnson's complaint that in metaphysical poetry "the most heterogeneous ideas are yoked by violence together." Certainly, poems like Donne's "Batter My Heart, Three-Personed God" clearly bring contexts together that are widely separated conceptually. In Donne's poem, however, the metaphorical exploration of human spirituality in violent and sexual terms not only produces powerful images, it also extends, within the brutal spaces of this audacious conceit, the conception of religious experience itself. In its deliberate, even brutal, exploration of religious experience in sexual, even masochistic, terms, Donne obliquely "explains" much of the implicit energy in ecstatic or charismatic religious movements and in so doing anticipates twentieth-century discoveries respecting structural correspondences among all forms of "peak experience."[4] The structure of the extended metaphor provides a disciplined framework for subliminal feeling, viscerally eloquent but formally inarticulate, to push thought into new territory. If the sensibility is acute and the poet's architectonic skills sufficiently sophisticated, Donne's art teaches us, feeling may sensuously *extend* thought. If this is the case then part of the aesthetic energy imparted to images in the unified sensibility becomes more readily comprehended, for it has not only imagic intensity but within this intensity is contained the excitement of new ideas. Perhaps this is what we ultimately mean by insight, a startling awareness in some new context of the relevance of something already subliminally known.

Something like this visceral sense, the sense in which we know something "in the bones," has been called the "tacit dimension"[5] by Michael Polanyi. In a series of books on "personal" knowledge, Polanyi, scientist and philosopher, tried to explore the sense in which people know more than they can tell and the sense in which that "more" is relied upon tacitly in a subsidiary way as explicit problems are formulated and solved in the focal awareness. In one important sense this personal component of knowledge may be seen as a deeply grounded inferential substratum that the visceral being develops naturally and often unselfconsciously. In Wittgensteinian terms we come to catch on to the rules at work in the games that constitute our form of life without having to learn them formally as rules; in Rylean terms we may acquire proficiency in the skill of following a rule without having the ability to represent that rule in propositional form.

Writing poetry is presented in "East Coker" as a military action against the unspoken and unsayable confusions of vague and undisciplined emotions. Of course the battleground motif with its notes of air raids and unruly squadrons is a neomusical conceit anticipating the last quartet, *Little Gidding*, in which the wartime theme is more fully developed in allusions to the London bombings and the English Civil War. It also serves conceptually here, however, to underscore the seriousness and the gravity of the problem of representing feeling for the writer: a continually frustrating imperative, but an imperative nonetheless, for as Eliot's Sweeney understands so well, there is no way to avoid language if one wishes to communicate. The writer's need to negotiate articulable pathways through the thickets of human feeling are in the last analysis always imperfect, always imprecise, and always essential.

The unavoidable imprecision involved in any attempt to make sense of feeling that Eliot here captures is relevant to the present study in two ways. The cognitive force of affect, the ways in which feeling may extend thought, can now be grafted onto the discussion of social intelligence in fiction in the last chapter. Certainly Jane Austen's ability to "feel into" the rules governing social meaning, as seen in the last chapter, represents the tacit emergence of insight, just as her ability to use those insights explicitly in her fiction marks the emergence of more focal knowledge. The other sense, how to make sense of our inner feeling life, will serve to introduce the principal theme of the present chapter: that in the exploration of the affective life of fictional characters some literary artists have produced knowledge that is of independent interest to contemporary behavioral science and the philosophy of mind. In particular, although emotions have traditionally been viewed as qualitatively discrete visceral events, during the past two decades most philosophers and psychologists have come to regard emotions as categories of feeling the contours of which are conceptually determined. The conceptual ingredients that discretely tinge feeling are a form of judgment philosophers call cognitive appraisals. On such an account to feel an emotion, as Richard Peters once argued, is *essentially* a cognitive event.

Insofar as the literary text routinely delimits the motivational and social contexts in which such appraisals are made, literature not only provides a rich source of insight into the possibilities of feeling but also illuminates the problems of understanding the fittingness of our emotions and communicating our emotional awareness more clearly and effectively. While Susanne K. Langer and her followers have long seen the crucial role that the arts, especially music, play in one's emotional life,[6] in presuming the traditional conception of emotion, Langer's view presents emotional meaning as a discrete nonliteral language and offers little *rational* traction on the problem of emotional development and explicit communication. Since the literary mode is linguistic and conceptual, however, it offers critical opportunities for rational discussion and analysis. In such a way this chapter will try to show that literary texts routinely provide readers with a medium to explore, refine, and extend sensibility.

Presenting the topic in this way further illustrates the manner in which the postmodern interest in the local and the particular in contrast to the general and universal, already discussed earlier in connection with Stephen Toulmin's *Cosmopolis*, may be pursued constructively through literary study. It also illustrates another of the sources of constructive postmodernism advanced in Chapter Three that is also strongly influenced by Toulmin's work: the strict separation of reason, as a mental or spiritual phenomenon in the philosophically "modern world view" inaugurated by Descartes, from the potentially frustrating and distorting influence of emotion. Toulmin finds a regrettable retrogression from Montaigne to Descartes: The vivid visceral curiosity at work in the humanist's sexually frank essay *On Some Verses of Virgil* is replaced by the philosopher's cautionary admonitions on subduing the untoward influence of the emotions in his *Treatise on the Passions*. Just as the Renaissance attitude reclaimed the classical one, the constructively postmodern may recapitulate both.

In suggesting a link at the level of visceral knowledge between the last chapter's subject of social intelligence in fiction and the present topic of emotional understanding, there is another important respect in which this chapter extends the work of the previous one. Adequately accounting for the theoretical interest embedded in the fiction of Jane Austen, Barbara Pym, and Anita Brookner required seeing that special kind of intellectual aptitude so evident in their work as a distinctive form of *social* intelligence. In this chapter another form of intelligent capability will similarly be developed in connection with writers as diverse as Henry James, E. M. Forster, and Marcel Proust. This kind of literary intelligence will be seen to be involved with the capacity to identify, make sense of, and represent the judgments and appraisals at work in the feeling lives of human beings. A still further aspect of connectedness between the present chapter and topics developed in earlier chapters is that its multifaceted approach to intellectual proficiency provides another illustration of the postmodern, especially the constructively postmodern, point of view.

POSTMODERN CONCEPTIONS OF INTELLIGENCE

In exploring the provenance of postmodern attitudes, previous chapters have identified the rejection of twentieth-century modernism's reductive pursuit of "essential" sources of cognitive and aesthetic value *and* the rejection of the modern philosophical fascination with formal logico-mathematical conceptions of rationality as two distinctive poles around which specific postmodern writers and positions are variously drawn. The modernist quest for essentialist doctrines in dance, philosophy, and the visual arts has been seen to be also relevant in the social and behavioral sciences. B. F. Skinner's stark reduction of the psychology of the human mind to a "black box" mediated only by the exigent rewards and punishments of operant conditioning is seen paralleled in the modernist sociology of Talcott Parsons, wherein all social roles and institutions are expressed neatly and precisely in terms of functional differentiation.

This reductionist modernist imperative may also be observed in the history of "intelligence" as a psychological construct. At about the same time Ezra Pound, Gertrude Stein, James Joyce, and Ernest Hemingway were in Paris consolidating the advances of the first wave of literary modernism and Walter Gropius, Mies van der Rohe, and other Bauhaus thinkers were asserting a core conceptual unity among all the creative arts under the primacy of architecture, a professor of psychology at University College in London, Charles Spearman, was completing work on a comparably "modernist" analysis of intelligence. Although it might have surprised Spearman to hear his work discussed in terms of the artistic *avant garde*, that work, *Abilities of Man*, published in 1927, represented Spearman's similarly reductive attempt to discover a "general intelligence factor" or simply a "g" that might underlie all differences in all forms of cognitive ability. Spearman reasoned that if there existed such a general intellectual engine for problem solving and the manipulation of formal relations, then it should be possible to find this factor at work across a wide variety of cognitive tests given to a large experimental sample.

The method of comparison used by Spearman was a form of correlational analysis. Although there is no causal chain implied in correlational analyses, they do measure quite accurately the extent to which two sets of numbers vary together. Two variables with a correlation coefficient of 1.0 vary in a one-to-one, perfect relationship, while a correlation of 0 would indicate that the two sets of numbers display no statistical correspondence at all. Correlations of .3 to .7 may be very significant in certain sample sizes, and Spearman's analysis of his data routinely resulted in correlation coefficients in this range. These findings encouraged Spearman to develop a two-factor theory of intelligence: that a person's performance on any given test was partly a result of a general intellectual factor, g, with the remaining variance unaccounted for by the general factor "explained" statistically by the special aptitudes embedded in each specific instrument or unique kind of intelligence test.

Spearman held that the g factor was at work in all intellectual tasks through what he called the qualitative principles of cognition. These cognitive principles included proficiency in the apprehension of experience, the eduction of relations, and the eduction of correlates. Apprehension figured in Spearman's theory not only as a perceptual skill but also involved the extent to which a person could understand the perceptions themselves, while the eduction of relations involved discovering relationships among those perceptual experiences and the extent to which a person could subsume novel experiential situations into ongoing structures of understanding. The eduction of correlates concept represents for Spearman the ability to apply rules inferred in one range of cases to a novel, but similar, case.[7]

Important caveats should be entered at this point, however. The statistically sophisticated form of correlational analysis developed by Spearman, called factor analysis, is capable only of establishing mathematical relationships between variables *as sets of numbers*. In no way is it capable of establishing relationships between what the variables are constructed to measure. These constructs must be independently shown to measure what the psychometrician takes them to measure. Establishing this kind of construct validity is entirely outside the scope of statistical analysis and very difficult to achieve satisfactorily. For this reason it is common in modern psychometrics to define constructs "operationally," tying the validity of the construct to the specific instrument involved in measuring it. In such operational definitions, the actual meaning of "intelligence" at work in a given intelligence test is precisely *whatever* behaviors are exhibited and recorded by a subject when taking it. A tidy approach, but one that leaves two important questions completely unanswered. First, we may ask with complete sincerity why an investigator like Spearman thinks his findings have anything to do with those prior ordinary notions of intelligence that have prompted scientific interest in its measurement. Second, we may also inquire of Spearman's findings, based as they were on many different instruments, why the g factor discerned therein has anything to do with the same prior, ordinary notions of intelligence. The g factor uncovered in correlational analysis could easily and plausibly be understood as a general test-taking competency; even more precisely still, it could simply involve proficiency in a certain kind of general test-taking competency, skewed heavily in the direction of a logico-mathematical, modern model of rational performance and a very particular (implicit and situational) set of learned historical, social, and cultural mediating variables.

The internal problems of Spearman's model of general intelligence began to emerge in the work of Louis Thurstone, a distinguished research professor of psychology at the University of Chicago and later at the University of North Carolina, who had begun his career in science as a laboratory assistant to Thomas Edison. His contributions to pyschometrics were formidable, creating the foundation for today's aptitude and achievement tests and the basis for contemporary methods of assessing attitudes and opinions. His *Factorial Studies of Intelligence*, published in 1941, applied a stronger statistical procedure than Spearman's that he had pioneered, multiple factor analysis, to a battery of test results from fifty-six tests given to 218 college students. Multiple factor analysis, which discerns relations among *sets* of variables, identified seven distinct factors at work in the sample. He named these factors verbal comprehension, verbal fluency, number, spatial visualization, memory, reasoning, and perceptual speed. Thurstone believed these findings contradicted Spearman's hypothesized g factor, while Spearman defended his findings by criticizing the homogeneity of Thurstone's test subjects and the great similarities among the tests he had used.

In identifying seven factors Thurstone did in fact begin to challenge the modernist view, although his work was itself not immune to the same quietly subversive problems of construct validity that have been seen to make mischief in Spearman's view. Notwithstanding those immanent problems there were further theoretical attempts to reconcile Thurstone's findings with the possibility of a general intelligence factor. H. J. Eisenk later suggested that a second g-factor analysis could be done on Thurstone's seven-factor data. If this analysis found one common statistical factor, then Spearman's hypothesis would be still viable, and if the seven factors could be shown statistically to yield such a second-order factor in common, then this factor could rightly be conceived as general intelligence.

Such an analysis was performed by James Cattell, who obtained not one, but two factors, which were in turn confirmed with a factor analysis of his own data based on his own tests. These factors were named "gf" for fluid intelligence and "gc" for crystallized intelligence. According to Cattell, and this move does begin to achieve some traction on the validity issue, gc depends on gf, with the fluid gc representing native ability and the potential to learn and solve problems and the crystallized gf representing the situationally specific and learned intellectual skills. Fluid intelligence supplies the native ability that in actual social and symbolic environments is "crystallized" in acquired skillful behaviors.

In the 1960s, J. P. Guilford comprehensively reviewed the literature on intelligence and psychometrics and concluded that there was insufficient evidence to support the hierarchical factor-analytical models of intelligence. His review revealed that many different factors had been variously reported and that there were clear conflicts concerning the existence of g, as well as problems of internal statistical consistency across the studies surveyed. He concluded that a two-dimensional hierarchical model could not adequately depict the structure of intellect and developed a "morphological" model, a cross-classification of phenomena with intersecting categories rather than categories within categories. The model Guilford developed ultimately presented 120 possible human abilities and was intentionally left open in anticipation of the need to add further categories. For Guilford, an intellectual factor results when any one of five operations combines with any one of six products and any one of four content areas.

By the 1970s even those psychometricians wedded to a factor-analytical framework for understanding intelligence, like P. E. Vernon, were losing some confidence in the explanatory power of a general intelligence factor. Vernon's research was based upon factor analyses conducted with test data from British army and navy conscript recruits. The model he developed postulates an underlying g factor but also acknowledges major group factors, which he called "V:ed" and "K:m." The major group factor, V:ed, embodies such minor group factors as verbal, numerical, and educational factors, while the K:m factor contains practical, mechanical, spatial, and physical factors. Vernon theorized that intelligence corresponds to the general level and complexity of a person's "schemata," conceptual or cognitive frameworks that structure experiential possibilities and that are cumulatively built up over a lifetime. Innate ability in human beings limits the ability to acquire schemata, while persons with a large stock of perceptual schemata can build more complex and flexible schemata. If the environment is stimulating, the individual will increase the complexity and flexibility of such perceptual possibilities.

Vernon's introduction of culturally informed and learned schemata is amplified in R. J. Sternberg's *Beyond I. Q.: A Triarchic Theory of Intelligence*, in which no one criterion is held satisfactorily to explain the complexities of the phenomena of intelligent performance. Sternberg saw the pursuit of an underlying g to be understandable, but he cautioned against the dangers of reductionism. In his triarchic theory, speed of component execution, accuracy of component execution, and the ability to deal with novelty, automize information processing, and bring the components of intelligence to bear upon practical situations are all different aspects of intelligence. No person is likely to be extremely good or bad in all these respects of problem solving; what is of interest, therefore, is the "profile" of intelligent performance that person exhibits, rather than any single score. In fact, any single score that attempts to summarize everything involved in intelligent performance will inevitably obscure the interesting and significant patterns it necessarily contains. The three parts of Sternberg's postmodern theory deal with three aspects of the complexity of intelligent performance: componential, experiential, and contextual. Such a multifaceted and contextualized view enables the profiles it produces to include practical aspects of behavior that enable people to adapt to changing environments. In addition to the componential intelligence (the process by which people identify problems, determine strategies for solving them, allocate and manage relevant resources, and execute their performance), experiential intelligence and contextual intelligence provide richly detailed, local and particular, frameworks for the analysis of intelligence.

With the publication of Howard Gardner's *Frames of Mind: The Theory of Multiple Intelligences* in 1983, the pursuit of a single underlying factor in intelligence was completely abandoned. Not only is the pursuit of such a factor seen to be misguided in Gardner: but unlike other critics of g, who sympathetically understood the quest, Gardner views intelligent performance to be necessarily a matter of multiple and discrete modalities of intelligent performance. Not only will specific strategies vary across people, but the very nature of the cognitive materials involved will vary dramatically in different people performing equally competently in the same intellectual tasks.

In choosing to study the particularities of individual people solving real problems and producing actual intellectual achievements in contexts that are fully naturalistic and thereby allow people to show their uniquely best cognitive performances, Gardner has been able to identify seven "intelligences" instead of the one previously so intently pursued. In addition to those forms of intellectual competency normally stressed in various I. Q. tests (but again which in Gardner are presented as discrete intelligences rather than simply components) like linguistic, logical-mathematical, and spatial, Gardner posits a bodily-kinesthetic intelligence in which the body is integrally at work in purposeful action or expression. If some people are predisposed to approach intellectual problems within a bodily or kinesthetic framework, other people might do so with reference to sound, rhythm, and other aspects of what Gardner calls the "musical" intelligence. Still other people might be inclined to orient themselves cognitively with reference to what Gardner has called the "personal" intelligences. Here, as discussed in the previous chapter, Gardner detects two discrete streams of intelligence, the interpersonal and intrapersonal Intelligences. The notion of social intelligence developed in the previous chapter is significantly different from Gardner's interpersonal intelligence, but the notion of emotional intelligence to be developed here is much closer to his intrapersonal intelligence. The justification for a different term will become clearer once the concept of emotion is analyzed more fully. At this point, however, it should be clear that in creating a structurally ambivalent model of human intelligence whose multifarious pathways encourage the appreciation of diversity and complexity, Gardner's theory may be regarded as a fully postmodern development. Insofar as it points to a more productive way of dealing systematically with the phenomena of intelligent performance, it may also be seen to be a constructive one.

EMOTION AS THOUGHT IN FEELING

Having treated the "intelligence" side of emotional intelligence from a postmodern perspective, the discussion of thought and feeling may be resumed. Ancient and Renaissance sensibilities saw the interplay of what we would call cognition and affect in positive terms, while the modern view looks upon emotion as a potentially corrupting influence on "right thinking" that reason must prudently keep in check. It should not surprise, therefore, that the postmodern temperament often looks with favor at the productive interaction of thought and feeling. As early as 1910, a very unmodernist E. M. Forster devoted an entire novel to the theme of connecting emotion and thought. Expressed as the imperative, "Only connect,"[8] Forster's opening epigram to *Howards End* quotes the favorite theme of the novel's Margaret Schlegel, whose ambition it is to bring the more prosaic reason into fertile contact with feeling in the belief that joining the "prose" to the passion in human experience is essential for genuine human integrity. Forster would have been gratified by contemporary work on emotion, for easily the most compelling theme in this work, both psychological and philosophical, is the "participation" in various ways of cognition in the realm of affect and the healthy ways in which such interpenetration may lead to fuller and richer thoughts and feelings.

In an effort to summarize the present state of thinking in psychology and cognitive studies with respect to the idea of emotion, George Mandler stresses the shift, already discussed here in connection with the "modernism" of the psychological construct of intelligence, from the behaviorist's "implicit dictum against complex theory"[9] toward renewed interest in more richly textured accounts among the cognitive psychologists. Reaching strong positions in most university departments in the 1970s and all but eclipsing behaviorists toward the end of the century, cognitive psychologists actively embrace, in an appropriately postmodern fashion, theories that "implicate the knowledge and thought of the organism as determinants of action and experience."[10] Inevitably, along with such renewed interest in the complexities of thought and knowledge "came a concern with cognitive aspects of emotion."[11] Mandler finds the work of Stanley Schachter at Columbia University in the early 1970s of central importance to the contemporary psychological consensus on the nature of emotion, in that for Schachter, "visceral arousal was seen as a necessary condition for emotional experience, but the quality of the emotion depended upon cognitive, perceptual evaluations of the external world and the internal state."[12]

The same "concatenation of visceral arousal and cognitive arousal"[13] that characterizes the consensus in psychology may be seen paralleled in the philosophy of mind. Ronald de Sousa's work on *The Rationality of Emotion* is massively illustrative of the contemporary philosopher's appreciation of the complexities of human beings' emotional lives. "Emotions," de Sousa acknowledges, "are the function where mind and body most closely and mysteriously interact."[14] Through several hundred pages of text de Sousa illustrates the many different ways in which conceptions of emotion philosophically approach these intimate mysteries. His own very valuable perspective on these matters is of particular relevance to the present study, for he views literature as an exemplary source of emotional meanings. The significance of a given emotion arises in what de Sousa calls a "paradigm scenario," by which he means an original defining "drama" in experience. Such paradigm scenarios are vividly evocative and therefore may be seen to embody a type of situation that we learn to "feel" in a certain way. Much in the same way we catch on the meanings of linguistic phenomena, "emotions have a semantics that derives from paradigm scenarios in terms of which our emotional repertoire is learned and the formal objects of our emotion fixed."[15] These basic repertoires of emotions are reinforced imaginatively by stories, works of art, and popular culture and later may be supplemented and refined by literature, reminding us of Iris Murdoch's view of literature as "an education in how to picture and understand human situations."[16]

Although there is much relevance in de Sousa to the ways in which the literary sensibility is capable of informing our understanding of emotion, it is another, less creatively articulated but equally relevant position that will form the framework for the present discussion. For Richard Peters, emotions are linked logically to the cognitive appraisals that, in his view, importantly constitute them. Appraisals are a class of cognitions that are involved whenever we see a situation in some evaluative light; they express judgments about situations under a variety of aspects that may be considered agreeable or beneficial, or their contraries, in a variety of ways. As Peters says:

> To feel *fear* is, for instance, to see a situation as dangerous; to feel pride *is* to see with pleasure something as mine or as something I have had a hand in bringing about. Envy is connected with seeing someone as possessing what we want, jealousy with seeing someone as possessing something or someone to which or whom we think we have a right.[17]

The different appraisals one may make of a given external situation may result in different emotions being felt. Seeing a situation as threatening means fear; seeing the same situation as thwarting one's purposes means anger.

In making a strong claim about the emotions as forms of cognition, Peters is not saying that the emotion, although constituted by its appraisals, is an exclusively cognitive event. Of course the emotions have an inner, visceral reality, but his claim is that these visceral factors do not identify the different emotions. Consider, for example, the differences between the emotions of remorse and regret. It may be very difficult to summon up a distinctive affective state for each of these feelings, but it is easy to see that they are quite distinct emotions. Peters would say that the distinction lies in the cognitive contours of the emotions, the appraisals that constitute each one, with regret involving a judgment that an unfortunate state of affairs would have been better never happening. Remorse, on the other hand, involves that judgment certainly, but also includes an appraisal linking the unfortunate state of affairs to one's own culpability. One is implicated morally in a situation whose appraisal constitutes remorse, while regret simply does not involve this further judgment.

Some very interesting conclusions flow from Peters's account. First as emotions are constituted by cognitive appraisals or judgments, it makes good sense to ask whether a given emotional response is warranted or unwarranted in a given circumstance. It may be that an insufficiently careful analysis of a situation results in a judgment that a specific social situation is thwarting one's ambitions, and anger is felt when in fact the impediment is due to a simple misunderstanding. As such there is some scope for the critical evaluation of our appraisals, some rational traction on emotional response. Instead of seeing, in proper modern philosophical terms, reason at odds with emotion, Peters's view opens the possibility for meaningful and productive commerce between thought and feeling. There are two fundamental ways in which one's emotional responses may be refined. First, we may become more proficient in evaluating situations critically and understanding what precisely is happening in our various social, physical, and symbolic environments. Education may have a critical role here in that when it is properly conducted, it initiates one into the forms of knowledge and understanding necessary for developing useful representations of our various environments. In addition to developing such knowledge bases, education may also have an important methodological role to play in terms of developing specific sets of critical thinking skills, so that the knowledge had may be most productively applied in given situations.

In addition to assessing situations more accurately, or at least coming to acknowledge evaluative possibilities other than a spontaneous one, a second way in which our emotional responses may be refined lies in expanding the repertoire of possible emotional appraisals. Although it may sound odd at first, it may be that quite a few emotions may only be felt by one who has first acquired the conceptual prerequisites necessary to make a given appraisal, and here the literary sensibility is of first importance:

> To enter into the descriptions of a writer such as . . . George Eliot is to have one's capacity for making appraisals extended. We tend to think too much of human beings as having the capacity for making discriminations which are put into words by others. It is nearer the truth to say that we learn to make the discriminations by entering into the descriptions.[18]

Just how much we may learn about the possibilities of feeling from literary texts is what the remainder of this chapter will attempt to show, and it is a very rich vein to tap. The emotions are highly complex and, as Peters rightly observes, "it may . . . take a whole novel like *Howards End* to explore the range of an emotion like indignation."[19]

INDIGNATION IN FORSTER

The first matter of business will be to return to E. M. Forster and *Howards End* to attempt to discover what this novel may teach us about the nature and possibilities of indignation. Although often discussed as the quintessential Bloomsbury novel in its limpid, finely textured prose, there is an implicit moral toughness in *Howards End* that reaches out for more sophisticated philosophical analysis. Perhaps this is why Peters's tantalizing invitation to consider the intellectual parameters of appraisals connected with "indignation" may be so profitably taken up, for the most important lesson Forster has to teach us in connection with this emotion is that, at its conceptual

core, an undeniable and unavoidable moral judgment must be formulated. Close attention to the normative contexts embedded in the
actual instances in which indignation is at work substantively in the
novel will show that this moral judgment is often rashly and inap-
propriately reached and that the special indignation it inspires is
both symptom and cause of an especially invidious form of injus-
tice.

Forster's childhood is connected through his influential great-aunt
and benefactress, Marianne Thornton, to a militantly moral environment, the Clapham Sect, a group of evangelical and anti-slave-
trade philanthropists. Marianne Thornton's father had been a lead-
ing member of this cause, and her legacy to Edward Morgan, both
moral and financial (she left him £8,000 in her will) may be taken as
evidence of an environment of social concern in which his continuing development was influenced. Although his father died shortly
after his birth, Forster's early childhood was a happy one at
Rooksnes, Stevenage, a house that he evokes so reverentially as
Howards End, the house so deeply and mysteriously steeped in an
authentically integrated human spirit in the novel to which it gives
its name. His public school years at Tonbridge were less pleasant,
however, and this experience provided him with another legacy,
which will be seen to work in *Howards End* harmoniously with the
moral one from his great-aunt: a firmly embedded dislike and dis-
trust of English public-school values. In the more sympathetic at-
mosphere of King's College, his years in Cambridge were much more
congenial; he was elected to an exclusive intellectual society, the
Apostles, and was drawn naturally to the Bloomsbury Group. After
a year of travel in Italy with his mother and a cruise to Greece, Forster
had sufficient material for his early novels, which satirized the attitudes of the English abroad. Satire, Fowler rightly observed, is a
moral genre; it aims to improve. Hence, it would be instructive also
to consider the improving tendencies of *The Longest Journey* and *A
Room with a View* in light of the account of indignation implicit in
Howards End. This implicit sense of indignation, scornful anger at
the hypocritical social displacement of genuine, grounded moral
integrity by conventional, class-based norms, is an important moral
center for *Howards End* and, together with the many individual epi-
sodes illustrating more conventional forms of indignation, thematically produces a unifying aesthetic and moral coherence in the work.

In *Howards End* the sisters Schlegel and their younger brother,
grown children of an affluent English mother and German idealist

father, live independently in London after their parents have both died. They become acquainted with Leonard Bast, a clerk of humble origins, at a concert when the younger sister Helen mistakenly walks off with Leonard's umbrella. At first Leonard is indignant when it appears to him that he has been the object of a confidence trick and declines to give his address to the older sister, Margaret, so that the umbrella may be returned, fearing further theft. Now it is Margaret who is indignant that this fellow would think of her in that way (it is an unjust appraisal) and otherwise arranges for Leonard to have his umbrella back. This comedy of appraisals is relieved when the sisters take an interest in Leonard, whose independent imagination and penchant for books pleases them.

Margaret Schlegel marries the widower Henry Wilcox long after Helen's very brief romantic attachment, while visiting the Wilcox home, Howards End, to his youngest son, Paul. Between the engagement and the death of Mrs. Wilcox, she and Margaret become sympathetic friends; shortly before her death Mrs. Wilcox makes it understood that Howards End should come to Margaret, a request the family ignores, indignantly and wrongly presuming inappropriate influence on the part of Margaret on Mrs. Wilcox. A "thoughtful" note to Margaret after Mrs. Wilcox's death inquiring if Mrs. Wilcox had promised her anything, to which Margaret replies negatively, serves to remove any reason for resentment but does not alter the family's intention of keeping the house nevertheless. After Margaret's marriage it is learned that Henry has had an affair with the woman now married to Leonard Bast and later that Helen has become pregnant through a brief liaison with the same Mr. Bast.

The ardent but fugitive "engagement" of the youthful, spontaneous Helen Schlegel with the youngest Wilcox son, Paul, while visiting Howards End is broken almost as soon as it commenced, but the letter Helen dispatches to her sister Margaret in London that announces the attachment is sufficient to send their aunt, Mrs. Munt, northward to Hertfordshire on a fact-finding mission. Mrs. Munt has a protective interest in the two women, as their parents are both deceased and since they have independent means and choose to live alone with their younger brother, Tibby. That Margaret receives another letter announcing the breaking of the engagement just after Mrs. Munt's train has left the station sets the scene for several instances of misunderstanding and indignation upon her arrival. One of these incidents, although apparently of little real consequence, when tapped for the sources of the indignation felt and expressed is most revealing. At the station Mrs. Munt is offered a lift to Howards End by the elder son Charles Wilcox, whom she has temporarily mistaken to be Paul, Helen's suitor.

But before they embark for Howards End, Charles is pointedly annoyed with a porter who is less than prompt in locating the parcel Charles had, in part, come to retrieve. Parcels do get misplaced, of course, but Charles reckons the delay is greater than necessary. He makes plain his prejudices in connection with the operation of the station in explaining matters to Mrs. Munt. He would, if he had his way, see that they all "should get the sack."[20] After some ritualistic fulmination with the porter, the porter produces the parcel and requests that Charles sign the receipt book. Charles first gruffly protests the necessity of providing his signature and then chastises the porter for not proffering a pencil with which the book might be signed. In driving off, Charles offers a final rebuke: "Remember, next time I report you to the station-master. My time's of value, though yours mayn't be."[21]

The transaction is vivid with the superficial signs of indignation. A person of social standing and means like Charles Wilcox should not need to put up with the silly formalities associated with a the job of a person in a porter's position; the very notion that there might be any question about his identity or truthfulness is insulting, hence the ventilation of annoyance and scorn. In terms of the relative severity of the two instances of misfeasance the porter might be guilty of committing in this scene—misplacing a parcel and failing to get the required signatures—one can imagine the porter being disciplined, if not discharged by his employers for allowing a parcel to leave the station without securing the appropriately completed receipts. But the simple fact of being implicated in a misplaced parcel, something for which he may not be personally responsible, is of far less consequence. Yet it is the porter's doing his job appropriately that occasions the verbal abuse. Almost to underscore the inappropriateness of Charles's gratuitous indignation, Forster follows the unjustified castigation of a worker for following his required procedures with Charles handing the porter a tip.

Here we see in Charles's behavior a form of indignation in which the dignity compromised is superficially claimed by right of social position and means. Its expression is a way of asserting those privileges, indeed also a means of enjoying the public spectacle of others whose lack of position obliges them to endure such a verbal assault. Viewed in this light, we can appreciate the special force of the tip:

clearly it is not for promptness, or special attention like providing a handy pen for Charles to use. Forster has us see it, at least in part, as a form of impersonal compensation for the public pleasure Charles might well take in asserting his status and confirming the insignificance of the porter as person through a vain, self-indulgent, and unjustified indignation.

It is not unlike the foolish indignation Charles's father Henry Wilcox later exhibits at the driver of a horse and cart who had the temerity to "interfere" with his car, apparently by crossing the road. Forster has prior to this scene established that Henry has a habit of driving recklessly at excessive speeds and has been caught in police speed traps before, hence the indignation Henry exhibits toward "a wretched horse and cart . . . [and] a fool of a driver,"[22] a combination that has ruined their journey. As Wilcox is appropriately insured the matter is of little significance except for the injury to Henry's view of his own importance. The fate of the unfortunate cart driver and horse, "being practically at right angles"[23] to Henry's colliding automobile, is of little apparent concern. Here again, Forster is quietly but effectively expressing his own indignation at the indifference of Wilcox to the injury of the cartman. As an additional note, the policeman at the scene of the accident, who concurs with Wilcox's assessment of the driver as a fool, may also be included in Forster's indignant scorn, in tugging a bit too obviously at his forelock in the presence of the wealthy Henry Wilcox.

Returning to Charles Wilcox and Mrs. Munt *en route* to Howards End, the pair stop at a shop to collect some goods for that house. Helen's aunt has now become clear about the identity of her traveling companion. In the process, however, Charles has learned for the first time about his brother's love-making to Helen. His first response is an expression of alarm and contempt at the suggestion that his brother has been dallying with the pretty niece. Although Mrs. Munt had come up to discourage the association, the indignant tone Charles uses, not unlike that addressed previously in the journey to the porter, spurs her to defend her niece's role in the relationship and then ultimately to blame everything on her unacceptable suitor. In this transaction, therefore, Forster may be seen to play one foolish variety of indignation against another and equally foolish one, in tones of rising audibility. For now Charles, revealingly sensitive to the shop assistants, says to Mrs. Munt, "Could you possibly lower your voice? The shopman will overhear."[24]

Perhaps the central individual example of indignation in *Howards End* occurs when Charles and his father hear of Helen's pregnancy. They are anxious to have the right thing done by her and to deal with her "seducer," the earlier mentioned Leonard Bast, as they think fit. Charles goes immediately to confer with Tibby, the sisters' ineffectual brother, but of course as a man he is therefore to be expected to take part in settling the matter. The conversation between the Margaret and Henry Wilcox on how the Wilcox men intend to proceed exhibits the brutal ingredients of such a settlement: a thrashing of Leonard by one or both of the Wilcox men. The grandly indignant tone Henry takes in this conversation with his wife is given a dapper dimension of hypocrisy in that Forster has already presented Henry Wilcox as a confessed adulterer himself. But in that case the equation of social class was inversely weighted. The thrashing eventually takes place, and it is in the commencement of this beating by Charles that Leonard Bast's weak heart stops; ruled guilty of manslaughter, Charles is sent to prison for three years.

We have seen indignation in a wide variety of settings throughout the novel, from the opening comedy of the umbrella through the grandly hypocritical indignation of Charles Wilcox at his unmarried sister-in-law's pregnancy. In each of these examples the case for justified indignation has been weakened by the apparent lack of willfulness on the part of the perceived offender. But there is a deeper sense in which they all mostly fail, and that is the sense in which the kind of "dignity" offended is itself morally problematic. Earlier there was reference to the implicit analysis of indignation that is the moral core of *Howards End*; and it is this analysis that undermines the justification for virtually all the instances of that emotion displayed throughout the book. Simply put, for Forster, genuine human dignity, what he calls humanity, has little to do with conventional representations of probity and propriety, but rather is grounded in integrity.

This humane moral wholeness is of course the object of Margaret Schlegel's dictum, "Only connect," that multicolored bridge that puts the formal cognitive principle in touch with enlivening feeling and compassion. Not only is it the theme of the novel, it is a symbolic subplot connecting Margaret to the first Mrs. Wilcox, and to the house, Howards End. For it is Howards End in which the connectedness between thought and feeling is rooted in the novel, just as the house in Stevenage that was its inspiration in Forster's own life had provided him a moral baseline. The spirit of humane integrity, its expression and its archetype, is the first Mrs. Wilcox whose first appearance in the novel occurs amid the vortex of sundry "indignations" surrounding the ephemeral courtship of Helen Schlegel and Paul Wilcox. These indignant responses have already been discussed, but the manner in which Forster presents Mrs. Wilcox to us sounds a deeply resonant chord:

> She approached . . . trailing noiselessly over the lawn, and there was actually a wisp of hay in her hands. She seemed to belong not to the young people and their motor, but to the house, and to the tree that overshadowed it. One knew that she worshipped the past, and that the instinctive wisdom the past alone can bestow had descended upon her.[25]

This "instinctive wisdom," the consolidation of understandings, mostly viscerally felt as instinctive impulses, is the source of Forster's humanity. Forster views this as the genuine source of the wisdom that we clumsily view as aristocratic, but this is a natural aristocracy that has nothing at all to do with the conditions of one's birth. "Highborn she might not be," Forster tells us, "but assuredly she cared about her ancestors, and let them help her. When she saw Charles angry, Paul frightened, and Mrs. Munt in tears, she heard her ancestors say: 'Separate those human beings who will hurt each other most. The rest can wait.'"[26] Those formalities which would preoccupy the attention of a conventionally "dignified" lady did not concern her. She did not inquire about details, nor did she artfully fail to notice that anything untoward had happened. Mindless of how a proper hostess would handle things, she simply and politely directs Helen to make her aunt comfortable in one of the upstairs rooms and she asks Paul to tell the cook that there will be one more for lunch than planned. Finally, upon Charles she bestows a kindly smile. Thus is Mrs. Wilcox presented as the spirit of an integrated, humane dignity, the integration of feeling, in the viscerally intelligent sense of Dewey, with thought and action. This compelling scene is emblematic of the connection that Forster holds to be at the core of moral being.

Howards End must continue to inspire this silently eloquent humanity. When Mrs. Wilcox is near death, she instructs her husband that Margaret Schlegel, who will ultimately succeed her as the second Mrs. Wilcox and in whom she detected a connected intelligence that might (in view of Margaret's superior facility with ideas and theories) enhance the efficacy of the house's humane impulse, is to inherit the house. Although quite a few subsequent, superficial "indignations" must first come to pass and the ineluctable interventions of the mysterious and Norne-like housekeeper, Miss Avery, must transpire, the house does ultimately come to Margaret Wilcox. First a home and refuge for her husband and herself, the house is later bequeathed to her outright. As the final connection in the novel is established, Margaret makes plain her intention of leaving the house to her nephew, who now lives in complete integrity with his mother Helen and the Wilcoxes in Howards End.

The locus of cognitive appraisals involved in an emotion like indignation, Forster shows us, is complex, having both superficial and more profound layers of moral judgment. Forster also show us how reflection on and evaluation of the appraisals we might spontaneously make in situations of potential personal indignation can yield significant insight into how we picture our social selves and the justness of these representations. Forster's analyses of indignation demonstrate clearly the role R. S. Peters anticipated for literary texts in improving the coherence of our emotional and moral lives. The more we understand the nature of the judgments surrounding an emotion, the wider the range of analyses we may undertake; the wider the range of analyses, the larger the set of opportunities for active participation in, and even direction of, our emotional lives. Forster demonstrates that the richness of situational presence in literature can be an impressive window onto the conceptual substrata of emotions.

In the same way that Forster's *Howards End* informs so cogently about indignation, a novel like *Lord Jim* could be viewed as a treatise on the appraisals associated with remorse and regret, with Conrad's textual anatomy of remorse exposing the appropriate moral issues as incisively as Forster does for indignation. There is an embarrassment of riches from which to choose, therefore, in illustrating the relevance of emotional intelligence in fiction to contemporary work on the emotions in psychology and philosophy, given the natural and finely textured ways in which human situations are presented in so many works of literature. Perhaps the most compelling emotional insights to be found in these texts, however, surround the ways in which the literary imagination has explored the most complex of human emotions, love: that congeries of forms of intimate, passionate, and affectionate attachment between people. It might be most instructive, therefore, to look very selectively at some of the distinctive kinds of appraisals at work in different instances of this emotion in literary texts. Two distinctively revealing perspectives on love will be considered in what follows: the measured, cultivated realization of affectionate affinity in Henry James and the more precipitate and passionate course of erotic excitement in Proust.

HENRY JAMES

In *The Portrait of a Lady*, the story a young woman of a remarkable sensibility joined to a keen intellectual appetite, James presents a closely analytical case study of the development and decay of a kind of love that is, in large part, cognitively achieved. Isabel Archer, an American heiress abroad to pursue the expansion of experience that the old cultures of Europe alone could properly facilitate, declines the marital proposals of a prosperous American entrepreneur and a British peer in favor of an alliance with the widower Gilbert Osmond, an expatriate American dilettante of subtle but unambitious talents. His very modest financial resources are husbanded judiciously and provide him and his daughter, Pansy, whose mother has died, with some scope for a life of tasteful gentility. The formation of this relationship is carefully directed, unbeknownst to Isabel, by another expatriate American, Madame Merle. Madame Merle is, in fact, the real mother of Pansy, and although their affair has long since ended, she and Osmond continue a close and psychologically intimate relationship. In "making" this marriage, Madame Merle is effectively pursuing the possibility of an advantageous marriage for Pansy at the suitable time, in that Isabel's fortune will move the Osmonds into a far more significant social situation.

Although there were contemporaneous complaints of the book being underplotted and overly "treated," the plot actually provides an almost perfect framework for exploring and representing the judgments and appraisals that initially coalesce in Isabel's love for Osmond and which ultimately are progressively undermined by Isabel's intelligence. Always incisive, her intellectual powers develop in the more socially complex environments of Europe to a more subtle and sophisticated degree. Her love for Osmond ends as it began, in the exercise of intelligence. Although there are intimations of a view of the more eager, passionate forms of human love in this portrait, as there are in other early and middle novels of Henry James, his considered treatment of this emotion is to be found deferred until his three last poetic novels. In *The Wings of the Dove*, the emotion is at the center of the seduction of the dying heiress Milly Theale by the impecunious English journalist, Merton Densher, an affair calculated and controlled by Densher's lover Kate Croy, who rightly believes that Milly will fall in love with Densher and leave him, upon her imminent death, an inheritance sufficient to support Kate's own amorous connection with the journalist. Likewise in *The Ambassadors* the key event prompting the righteous Mrs. Newsome's separate embassies to her son in Paris, that of Lambert Strether and later of Sara Newsome, is Chad Newsome's passionate relationship with the alluring Madame de Vionnet; while *The Golden Bowl* examines the same intense emotion as it plays between and among a father and his daughter and their spouses.

But the love of Isabel Archer for Gilbert Osmond is not of this heated variety. If the ancients understood anything about Eros or Venus it is that in the passionate forms of love, one is preoccupied with the intimate physical proximity of the beloved, which obsession may or may not be sexually expressed and whose power is neither increased or diminished for very long by sexual contact. It is the form of love that Lucretius analyzes so acutely in *De Rerum Naturum*, and in commencing this discussion it will be good to have this, its finest account, at hand. Lucretius proposes that "in love there is the hope that the flame of passion may be quenched by the same body that kindled it. But this runs . . . counter to the course of nature. This is the one thing of which the more we have, the more our breast burns with the . . . lust of having."[27] Apart from momentary respites, Venus teases and provokes lovers with impossible hungers that simply cannot be quenched:

> They cannot glut their eyes by gazing on the beloved form, however closely. Their hands glean nothing from those dainty limbs in their aimless roving over all the body. . . . Then comes the moment when with limbs entwined they pluck the flower of youth. Their bodies thrill with the presentiment of joy, and it is seed-time in the fields of Venus. Body clings greedily to body; moist lips are pressed on lips, and deep breaths are drawn through clenched teeth. But all to no purpose. One can glean nothing from the other, nor enter in and be wholly absorbed, body in body.

> ... At length, when the spate of lust is spent, there comes
> a slight intermission in the raging fever. But not for long.
> Soon the same frenzy returns. The fit is upon them once
> more.[28]

Little wonder that Lucretius, in proper Epicurean form, councils coping with the illusive imperatives of this emotion only when they simply cannot otherwise be avoided; when choice permits, it is far better to aim for the settled pleasure of *ataraxia*, that highest form of Epicurean pleasure, to be found in the freedom of the soul from disturbance, the true omega of human experience.

Although she does make positive appraisals of his appearance, Isabel's fondness for Osmond's physical form never rises to this high level of passionate preoccupation. The physical element is not presented by James as a central feature of Isabel's attachment to Osmond; he rather shows us how in this independent woman more discursive interests are at work in her growing affection for her future husband. First among these interests is Isabel's avid desire to extend her range of understanding and knowledge. It may seem odd to find that in this kind of love a primary engine is cognitive, but here we discover another important source of interpenetration between thought and feeling. In the earlier discussion of Donne, that poet's ability to use feeling to push thought into new conceptual territories was acknowledged to have independent epistemological significance, in addition to its literary interest. In James's account of Isabel Archer's love for Osmond can now be found a vivid example of thought pushing feeling forward into new *emotional* territory.

Isabel, it is clear, desires to know. Indeed, James presents this aspect of Isabel's character very early in the novel: "Isabel Archer was a young person of many theories; her imagination was remarkably active. It had been her fortune to possess a finer mind than most of the persons among whom her lot was cast; to have a larger perception of surrounding facts and to care for knowledge that was tinged with the unfamiliar."[29] To these cognitive predispositions may be added a measure of vanity in that she wishes sometimes "that she might find herself some day in a difficult position, so that she should have the pleasure of being as heroic as the occasion demanded."[30] Her rich capacity to be moved by sympathetic individuals to a kind of ennobling pity, she exhibits in conversation with Ralph Touchett:

Do you complain of Mr. Osmond because he is not rich? That is just what I like him for. I have fortunately money enough; I have never felt so thankful for it as to-day. There are moments when I should like to go and kneel down by your father's grave; he did perhaps a better thing than he knew when he put it in my power to marry a poor man— a man who has borne his poverty with such dignity, with such indifference.[31]

The development of Isabel's love for Osmond represents the gradual formation of appraisals respecting the cognitive interests that an involvement with him may be taken to further, the attractive risks inherent in negotiating an intimate relationship with a new, unknown type of character, and the judgments associated with seeing in this relationship with Osmond an opportunity for a sort of enlightened domestic philanthropy. The epistemological, sentimental, and self-indulgent appraisals that Isabel makes in these matters converge in the emotion of love.

The artistic center of the novel is in effect the story of the formation of these appraisals, the way their formation is "assisted" by the subtle treacheries of the darkly brilliant Madame Merle, and in the climax of the novel, the ways in which the very intellectual aptitude and energy that attract Isabel to Osmond also, as she detects more and more anomalies through her reflective exploration of her situation, progressively undermine the bases of these appraisals and thereby her love for him. The novel's central episode in Chapter 42, what James thought the strongest and best "thing" in the book, is fittingly (and audaciously) inert. In respect of dramatic action or even in terms of simple physical movement, Isabel only sits alone by the fire, long into the night and morning, *thinking*: slowly and carefully reconsidering and reevaluating the basis for her judgments concerning Osmond and beginning to raise to the level of conscious thought the significance of Madame Merle's role in her predicament, of which she had earlier had a sharply visceral presentiment. Returning from a walk in the Roman Campagna, Isabel enters her drawing-room and, just beyond its threshold, stops abruptly, "the reason for her doing so being that she had received an impression." This impression:

had, in strictness, nothing unprecedented; but she felt it as something new, and the soundlessness of her step gave her time to take in the scene before she interrupted it. Madame Merle was there in her bonnet, and Gilbert Osmond was talking to her; for a minute they were unaware she had come in. Isabel had often seen that before, certainly; but what she had not seen, or at least had not noticed, was that their colloquy had for the moment converted itself into a sort of familiar silence, from which she instantly perceived that her entrance would startle them. Madame Merle was standing on the rug, a little back from the fire; Osmond was in a deep chair, leaning back and looking at her. Her head was erect, as usual, but her eyes were bent on his. What struck Isabel first was that he was sitting while Madame Merle stood; there was an anomaly in this that arrested her. Then she perceived that they had arrived at a desultory pause in their exchange of ideas and were musing, face to face, with the freedom of old friends who sometimes exchange ideas without uttering them. There was nothing to shock in this; they were old friends in fact. But the thing made an image, lasting only a moment, like a sudden flicker of light. Their relative positions, their absorbed mutual gaze, struck her as something detected.[32]

Inquiry commences, John Dewey demonstrated in his *Logic*, when a person situationally detects an anomaly in some set of environing conditions, whether physical, symbolic, or social. This anomaly is detected as a felt quality and only resolved when sufficiently efficacious cognitive tools are successfully formulated and brought to bear on the situation. James has here provided a stunning example of how the process of inquiry may be initiated in ordinary situations and how its dynamics my usefully be studied in a literary text. A further example occurs in Chapter 31, which likewise involves Madame Merle. In this scene Isabel is viscerally alarmed by a shocking feeling of fright when a subtle moral point she makes, which Madame Merle's intelligence should instantly grasp, is not understood. The horrible possibility that Madame Merle may be more or less than she appears to be fills Isabel with a strange sense of foreboding. James is remarkably in touch with the power of visceral apprehension to promote the development of new cognitive understandings in *The Portrait of a Lady*. Elsewhere, we learn that Isabel is "studying," in the words of her cousin, Ralph Touchett, "human nature at close quarters"[33] as part of her quest for a wider and more systematic understanding of people. She is therefore impelled actively to seek out anomalies in the social situations through which she moves and is quick to register their images in her memory for later reflection. This pursuit of new knowledge makes a most interesting image; Osmond is seen as unique when compared with others in her acquaintance. Isabel's "mind contained no class which offered a natural place to Mr. Osmond—he was a specimen apart. Isabel did not say all these things to herself at the time; but she felt them, and afterwards they became distinct."[34]

We saw similar forms of inquiry implicitly at work in *Mansfield Park* earlier in this study, as Miss Crawford worked to sort out the semiotic anomalies at play in Fanny Price's social situation. Sorting out such situational anomalies in naturalistic contexts is now regarded as a fully appropriate subject for systematic empirical study. The relevance of James to this kind of study is perspicuous. In the process of developing his initial artistic conception of "a young woman affronting her destiny,"[35] James exemplifies an empirical approach to the analysis of character that is focused, subtle, and finely grained. The central importance of observation, point of view, and of a scientific approach to criticism in *The Portrait of a Lady* together could function quite coherently as a theoretical blueprint for the formation of contemporary qualitative methodologies. There is enough evidence of naturalistic, participatory observation in this work to support the contention that James may well have seen his own penetrating observations in the multitudinous dining rooms and drawing-rooms of New York and Europe, at least in part, as opportunities for developing systematic understanding of the elements and dynamics of interpersonal judgment and emotional awareness. Indeed the achingly perceptive and manipulative Madame Merle, one of the most brilliant women in fiction, is acknowledged by Gilbert Osmond to have a propensity for, and skill at, empirical investigation. "Pardon me," he observes to Madame Merle, "that isn't—the knowledge I impute to you—a common sort of wisdom. You've gained it in the right way—experimentally; you've compared an immense number of more or less impossible people with each other."[36] Madame Merle, for her part, is not shy about the uses to which such knowledge may politically be put. Bluntly uninterested in people as ends, the amoral Madame Merle admits, "I don't pretend to know what people are meant for.... I only know what I can do with them."[37] Osmond's sister, who will later be the independent "instrument" confirming Isabel's growing visceral hypotheses surrounding the true role of Madame Merle in her life, is not incorrect in proclaiming Madame Merle to be the true Machiavelli.

While Madame Merle actively experiments with people, Isabel's interest is more passive and therefore more morally sensible. As we have already seen, she tests the adequacy of her developing representations of character and motive not by manipulation but by careful observation within the uncontrived situations of her daily life. And she *reflects*. At the close of her ruminative vigil by the fire in Chapter 42, her mind is still in a state of "extraordinary activity," and:

> When the clock struck four she got up; she was going to bed at last, for the lamp had long since gone out and the candles burned down to their sockets. But even then she stopped again in the middle of the room and stood there gazing at a remembered vision—that of her husband and Madame Merle unconsciously and familiarly associated.[38]

From this point, as the complex appraisals that have commingled in one of the most cognitively achieved instances of love in literature begin to unravel, so too does that emotion gradually cease to characterize Isabel's feelings for Osmond.

PROUST

In coming to Proust, we move from one great investigator of sensibility to another. The great love affair of *Remembrance of Things Past* and the most subtle and unified section of that massive work occurs in the third part of the initial volume, *Swann's Way*. Here, in "Swann in Love," are the finely detailed particulars of the formation of a passionate attachment between Swann and the *demi-mondaine*, Odette de Crécy, and the development of an initially diffuse and inchoate feeling on the part of Swann into love of the most piquant and enthralling kind. Swann's drama of emotional commotion and its resolution is played out against the precise social comedy of the family Verdurin and its "little clan" of regular visitors. This "salon" of Madame Verdurin is maintained in the opulent, if somewhat vulgar and pretentious, parlors of her affluent bourgeois home. It is into this environment that Swann, a far more cultivated burgher with many points of entry to the upper classes, finds himself implicated as it provides a convenient pretext for seeing Odette, herself a stalwart of the little clan. The imperious Madame Verdurin tacitly insists on two articles of faith among her little "nucleus." They must all attend the Verdurins' social evenings to the virtual exclusion of all other social commitments, and more significantly, they must all confirm on demand, as it were, the Verdurins' disdain for those more fashionable or aristocratic circles from which they are effectively barred. These "bores" are held by the Verdurins in constant and unflattering contrast with the privileged members of their little group. The structural ironies attendant on such a vainly positioned salon provide Proust with abundant opportunities for sardonic observation and social farce. The introduction of the more intelligent and percipient Swann to the group by Odette provides even more subtle occasions for comic effect.

Swann had initially been introduced to Odette at the theater, by a friend who suggested that he might ultimately come to an amorous arrangement with this attractive woman. Swann certainly saw the attraction her appearance and personality might have for many men, but as in that other revealing study of the course of passionate love, *Of Human Bondage,* the emotion here does not commence with desire. Swann, a man of the world accustomed to indulging his sexual appetites quite freely, has erotic tastes in feminine appearance that do not lead directly to Odette at all. She is, alas, the wrong type completely. Neither the delicacy of her skin nor the prominence of her cheekbones inspired any physical desire in him. Indeed, initially she was even slightly repugnant.

Swann has known the pleasures of being in love many times, although as a younger man these romantic adventures had initially been instigated by physical desire for the type, so unlike Odette, that Swann continues to fancy. Now, as Proust's narrator Marcel observes, Odette begins ever so subtly to pursue the amorous attentions of Swann. When, for instance, he at last allowed her to visit his home, she said how happy she was to visit finally a house she had so longed to see. These commonplace things are said in a tone of voice that suggests Swann is far more significant to her than all of her other acquaintances. Speaking to him in this way, she appears to Swann demurely to presume a kind of romantic bond between them, which makes him smile. For, as Proust observes so acutely, the evidence of such an effect in a man of Swann's age and experience brings with it so many associations to the pleasures of being in love that it can ultimately inspire, through an intellectual process, desire itself.

As Odette's avowals of romantic interest in him grow, therefore, as she tells him how time seems not to pass until he permits her once again to visit him or as she shyly pleads with him to visit her just one time for tea, Swann gradually succumbs to her subtle blandishments: "And so, at an age when it would appear—since one seeks in love before everything else a subjective pleasure—that the taste for a woman's beauty must play the largest part in it, love may come into being, love of the most physical kind, without any foundation in desire."[39] What begins as a most desultory association with Odette now, through the introduction of novel cognitive ingredients reminiscent of past loves, undergoes a transformation in his mind. Swann's awareness—an awareness of the most explicit and cognitive kind—of the interest he has created in Odette through his own attentive charm and cultivated personality, is a judgment so connected cognitively to the other appraisals normally associated with a love prompted by desire that the evaluative light associated with this "complex" of appraisals begins to dawn on this undoubtedly charming and otherwise very attractive woman. In this nexus of familiar appraisals and associations, Swann begins to seek out and highlight features in her appearance and character that may indeed be represented imaginatively in more and more affectionate terms. Indeed, Swann eventually comes to prepare himself to meet Odette by creating a picture of her in his mind on which he could focus selectively, concentrating on those of her physical features that he finds attractive and excluding from his imaginative representations those many features he dislikes.

Drawn by Odette into the salon of Madame Verdurin, Swann hears there one evening a certain piece of music he had once heard before and which had made a memorable and complex aesthetic impression on him. He had subsequently been unsuccessful in determining its composer, but here at the Verdurins' the circle's young pianist performs the piece, a sonata by Vinteuil, whose "little phrase" of such significance in Swann's recollections is finally placed. The reemergence of this phrase in the presence of Odette causes Swann, now predisposed to find new ways of representing Odette to his own erotic imagination, to mingle all the evocative associations of this music with his developing reconstruction of Odette's image. Memory here, as a specific instance of the larger general theme in Proust, is reconfigured to promote the appraisals of desire. In this

Swann is much like others of us in his particular situation, in that we are impelled by love remembered to fortify the complex of appraisals now in play:

> We come to its aid, we falsify it by memory and by suggestion. Recognizing one of its symptoms, we remember and recreate the rest. Since we know its song, which is engraved on our hearts in its entirety, there is no need for a woman to repeat the opening strains—filled with the admiration which beauty inspires—for us to remember what follows.[40]

This process of the cognitive reconstruction of memory reaches its most complete realization when Swann "notices" a similarity between Odette and Botticelli's portrait of Zipporah, Jethro's daughter, from one of the Sistine frescoes. The similarity permits Swann to recast his mental image of Odette in the style of an Old Master. Through the mediating influence of Florentine art, Odette is linked imaginatively to regions of Swann's most precious aesthetic reveries and thereby elevated to a finer and more durable pedestal. This deliberate association is definitive in consolidating for Swann the formation of the emotion of love, for it now argues away the "problems" which Swann has had about her appearance, permitting him to "re-erect his estimate of her on the sure foundations of aesthetic principle."[41] Swann has now succeeded, through a highly cognitive process, in grounding his love for Odette in an unproblematic physical desire.

Once established, this fully realized, passionate love immediately begins to assert its shadow, as for the kind of passionate love Proust delimits so astutely in *Swann's Way*, jealousy is its constant dark companion. The craving for an impossibly exclusive possession of the beloved in the most passionate forms of amorous desire described so effectively by Lucretius is developed by Proust into a detailed anatomy of erotic pathology throughout the full course of *Remembrance of Things Past*. But the concern of the present discussion is with those incipient judgments implicated in the development of Swann's love for Odette. In moving through the complex cognitive appraisals Swann makes before his love for Odette is consolidated in desire, Proust has shown the substantial, active role cognitive activity has in the formation of this emotion. This analytical dissection of what may be taken to be, at least in part, Proust's own experience with this powerful emotion challenges one very well-entrenched piece of conventional wisdom. Pascal's aphorism that the heart has its reasons that reason never knows captures the thought that the ways of love are intractable and unknowable. Proust's treatment of Swann in love as well as James's study of Isabel Archer's very different kind of love for Osmond both show how the special kind of emotional intelligence at work in an empirically grounded but imaginatively reported kind of inquiry can in certain literary texts move the understanding of this emotion forward with some clarity and no little precision.

CONCLUSION

It has been suggested that the aspect of constructive postmodernism that treats of the reintegration of thought and feeling recapitulates the ancient and Renaissance attitudes toward these topics. An attempt has also been made to demonstrate and illustrate how this attitude is also is fully consistent with recent work in psychology and philosophy on the emotions. In proposing a form of "emotional intelligence," which may be seen at work in some literary texts, the special potential some novelists possess for delimiting the situational bases for cognitive judgments that impact directly on human emotional lives has been stressed. Together with the advent of theories of multiple intelligences in contemporary psychology, as well as related conceptions like the notions of social and emotional intelligence developed in this chapter and Chapter Five, such a view is fully consistent with the contemporary rejection of modernist models of intelligence, which stressed for many years the pursuit of a single factor in all intelligent behavior. While postmodern in its rejection of such a univalent "intelligent" source of presence, the view of intelligence illustrated here is also a constructive one, inasmuch as it views a conceptually layered notion of intelligence as a better explanatory model for the *complexities* of cognitive talent displayed across a wide variety of situational *contexts*. It serves also to underscore the importance of pursuing the development of what might be called a general account of literary intelligence, of which social and emotional intelligence would be only two kinds. A general account of literary intelligence would treat those forms of cognitive acuity involved imaginatively in mining and representing verbally the intricacies and particularities of all aspects of human sensibility.

NOTES

1. T. S. Eliot, "The Metaphysical Poets," in *Selected Prose of T. S. Eliot*, ed. Frank Kermode (New York: Harcourt Brace Jovanovich, 1975), p. 64.

2. Ibid., p. 63.

3. Ibid., p. 66.

4. See Abraham Maslow, *Religions, Values, and Peak-Experiences* (New York: Viking Press, 1970), for a treatment of the structural correspondences among all forms of "peak experience."

5. Further discussion of Michael Polanyi's conception of implicit knowledge may be found in his *Personal Knowledge: Towards a Post-Critical Philosophy* (London: Routledge & Kegan Paul, 1958) and *The Tacit Dimension* (Garden City, N.Y.: Doubleday, 1966).

6. Susanne K. Langer's view of emotion may be pursued especially in her *Feeling and Form: A Theory of Art* (London: Routledge & Kegan Paul, 1953) and *Philosophy in a New Key: A Study in the Symbolism of Reason, Rite, and Art* (Cambridge: Harvard University Press, 1957).

7. The transition from modern to postmodern conceptions of intelligence may be followed more closely in the following sources: Charles Edward Spearman, *Abilities of Man: Their Nature and Measurement* (London: Macmillan and Co., Limited, 1927), and Louis Leon Thurstone, *Factorial Studies of Intelligence* (Chicago: University of Chicago Press, 1941).

8. E. M. Forster, *Howards End*, in *A Room with a View* and *Howards End* (New York: Modern Library, 1993), p. 213.

9. George Mandler, "Emotion," in *Oxford Companion to the Mind*, ed. Richard L. Gregory (Oxford: Oxford University Press, 1987), p. 219.

10. Ibid., p. 220.

11. Ibid.

12. Ibid.

13. Ibid.

14. Ronald de Sousa, *The Rationality of Emotion* (Cambridge, Mass.: MIT Press, 1987), p. xvi.

15. Ibid., p. 171.

16. Ibid., p. 184.

17. R. S. Peters, "The Education of the Emotions," in *Education and the Development of Reason*, ed. R. F. Dearden, P. H. Hirst, and R. S. Peters (London: Routledge & Kegan Paul, 1972), p. 467.

18. Ibid., p. 476.

19. Ibid.

20. Forster, *Howards End*, p. 227.

21. Ibid., p. 228.

22. Ibid., p. 293.

23. Ibid.

24. Ibid., p. 231.

25. Ibid., pp. 232–33.

26. Ibid., p. 233.

27. Lucretius, *De Rerum Naturum*, trans. R. E. Latham (Harmondsworth, Middlesex, England: Penguin Books, 1951), p. 164.

28. Ibid., pp. 164–5.

29. Henry James, *The Portrait of a Lady* (London: Oxford University Press, 1947), p. 51.

30. Ibid., p. 53.

31. Ibid., p. 375.

32. Ibid., pp. 442–43.

33. Ibid., p. 297.

34. Henry James, *The Portrait of a Lady* (New York: Library of America, 1985), p. 459.

35. Henry James, preface to *The Portrait of a Lady* (London: Oxford University Press, 1947), p. xx.

36. Ibid., p. 257.

37. Ibid., p. 259.

38. Ibid., p. 473.

39. Marcel Proust, *Swann's Way*, trans. C. K. Scott Moncrieff and Terence Kilmartin (Franklin Center, Pa.: Franklin Library, 1983), p. 226.

40. Ibid.

41. Ibid., p. 257.

Bibliography

Austen, Jane. *Mansfield Park*. London: Richard Bentley & Son, 1892.

Austen-Leigh, William, and Richard Arthur Austen-Leigh. *Jane Austen: A Family Record*. London: Macmillan, 1989.

Baudrillard, Jean. *Selected Writings*. Edited by Mark Poster. Stanford, Calif.: Stanford University Press, 1988.

———. *Simulacra and Simulation*. Translated by Sheila Faria Glaser. Ann Arbor: University of Michigan Press, 1994.

Blair, Fredrika. *Isadora: Portrait of the Artist as a Woman*. New York: McGraw-Hill, 1986.

Brookner, Anita. *Hotel du Lac*. London: Jonathan Cape, 1984.

Casement, William. *The Great Canon Controversy: The Battle of the Books in Higher Education*. New Brunswick: Transaction Publishers, 1966.

Cattell, James M. *An Education in Psychology*. Cambridge, Mass.: MIT Press, 1981.

Derrida, Jacques. *Of Grammatology*. Translated by G. C. Spivak. Baltimore: Johns Hopkins University Press, 1974.

———. *Positions*. Translated by Alan Bass. Chicago: University of Chicago Press, 1981.

Descartes, René. *Discourse on the Method of Rightly Conducting the Reason and Seeking Truth in the Field of Science*. Translated by Laurence J. Lafleur. New York: Bobbs-Merrill Company, 1960.

———. *Philosophical Writings*. London: Macmillan, 1952.

de Sousa, Ronald. *The Rationality of Emotion*. Cambridge, Mass.: MIT Press, 1987.

Dewey, John. *Art as Experience*. New York: G. P. Putnam's Sons, 1980.

————. *Logic: The Theory of Inquiry*. New York: Holt, Rinehart and Winston, 1938.

————. *The Quest for Certainty: A Study of the Relation of Knowledge and Action*. New York: Capricorn, 1960.

Donne, John. *Divine Poems*. Edited by Helen Gardner. Oxford: Clarendon Press, 1952.

Duncan, Isadora. *My Life*. New York: Horace Liveright, 1927.

Dworkin, R. M. *Life's Dominion: An Argument about Abortion, Euthanasia, and Individual Freedom*. New York: Knopf, 1993.

Eagleton, Terry. *The Illusions of Postmodernism*. Oxford: Blackwell, 1996.

Eliot, T. S. *Complete Poems and Plays, 1909–1950*. New York: Harcourt, Brace & World, 1971.

————. *Four Quartets*. New York: Harcourt, Brace and Company, 1943.

————. "The Metaphysical Poets." In *Selected Prose of T. S. Eliot*, edited by Frank Kermode. New York: Harcourt Brace Jovanovich, 1975.

Fenollosa, Ernest. *The Chinese Written Character as a Medium for Poetry*. San Francisco: City Lights Books, 1936.

Fenollosa, Mary. Preface to *Epochs of Chinese and Japanese Art*, by Ernest Fenollosa. New York: Dover Books, 1963.

Fielding, Nigel. "Ethnography." In *Researching Social Life*, edited by Nigel Gilbert. London: Sage Publications, 1993.

Forster, E. M. *The Longest Journey*. New York: Knopf, 1922.

————. *A Room with a View* and *Howards End*. New York: Modern Library, 1993.

Freud, Sigmund. *Civilization and Its Discontents*. Translated by Joan Riviere. London: Hogarth Press, 1963.

Gardner, Howard. *Frames of Mind: The Theory of Multiple Intelligences*. New York: Basic Books, 1983.

Garfinkel, Harold. *Studies in Ethnomethodology*. Englewood Cliffs, N.J.: Prentice-Hall, 1967.

Geertz, Clifford. *The Interpretation of Cultures*. New York: Basic Books, 1973.

Goffman, Erving. *Presentation of Self in Everyday Life*. Garden City, N.Y.: Anchor, 1959.

Grant, Gail. *Technical Manual and Dictionary of Classical Ballet*, 2nd ed. New York: Dover, 1967.

Green, Thomas F. *The Activities of Teaching*. New York: McGraw-Hill, 1971.

Grierson, Herbert John Clifford. *Metaphysical Lyrics & Poems of the Seventeenth Century, Donne to Butler*. Oxford: Clarendon Press, 1925.

Guilford, J. P. *Creative Talents: Their Nature, Uses, and Development*. Buffalo, N.Y.: Bearley Ltd., 1986.

Hamlyn, D. W. "Epistemology and Conceptual Development." In *Cognitive Development and Epistemology*, edited by Theodore Mischel. New York: Academic Press, 1971.

Hartman, Geoffrey. *Criticism in the Wilderness*. New Haven, Conn.: Yale University Press, 1980.

Holt, Hazel. *A Lot to Ask: A Life of Barbara Pym*. London: Macmillan, 1990.

Hulme, T. E. "Romanticism and Classicism." In *Prose Keys to Modern Poetry*, edited by Karl Shapiro. Evanston, Ill.: Harper & Row, 1962.

Husserl, Edmund. *Ideas Pertaining to a Pure Phenomenology and to a Phenomenological Philosophy*. Translated by F. Kersten. Dordrecht, The Netherlands: Kluwer Academic Publishers, 1983.

James, Henry. *The Portrait of a Lady*. London: Oxford University Press, 1947.

———. *The Portrait of a Lady*. New York: Library of America, 1985.

Janik, Allan, and Stephen Toulmin. *Wittgenstein's Vienna*. New York: Simon and Schuster, 1973.

Jonsen, Albert R., and Stephen Toulmin. *The Abuse of Casuistry: A History of Moral Reasoning*. Berkeley: University of California Press, 1988.

Kempson, Ruth M. "Semantics, Pragmatics, and Natural-Language Interpretation." In *The Handbook of Contemporary Semantic Theory*, edited by Shalom Lappin. Oxford: Blackwell, 1996.

Langer, Susanne K. *Feeling and Form: A Theory of Art*. London: Routledge & Kegan Paul, 1953.

———. *Philosophy in a New Key: A Study in the Symbolism of Reason, Rite, and Art*. Cambridge: Harvard University Press, 1957.

Leavis, F. R. *The Great Tradition*. London: Chatto & Windus, 1948.

Lévi-Strauss, Claude. *Conversations with Claude Lévi-Strauss*. Translated by Paula Wissing. Chicago: University of Chicago Press, 1991.

———. *Myth and Meaning*. Toronto: University of Toronto Press, 1978.

Lucretius. *De Rerum Naturum*. Translated by R. E. Latham. Harmondsworth, Middlesex, England: Penguin Books, 1951.

Lyotard, Jean-François. *The Postmodern Condition: A Report on Knowledge*. Translated by Geoff Bennington and Brian Massumi. Minneapolis: University of Minnesota Press, 1993.

Mandler, George. "Emotion." In *Oxford Companion to the Mind*, edited by Richard L. Gregory. Oxford: Oxford University Press, 1987.

Maslow, Abraham. *Religions, Values, and Peak-Experiences*. New York: Viking Press, 1970.

Pepper, Stephen C. *World Hypotheses*. Berkeley: University of California Press, 1942.

Peshkin, Alan, and Elliot Eisner. *Qualitative Inquiry in Education: The Continuing Debate*. New York: Teachers College Press, 1990.

Peters, R. S. "The Education of the Emotions." In *Education and the Development of Reason*, edited by R. F. Dearden, P. H. Hirst, and R. S. Peters. London: Routledge & Kegan Paul, 1972.

Polanyi, Michael. *Personal Knowledge: Towards a Post-Critical Philosophy*. London: Routledge & Kegan Paul, 1958.

―――. *The Tacit Dimension*. Garden City, N.Y.: Doubleday, 1966.

Pound, Ezra. *Literary Essays*. Edited by T. S. Eliot. New York: New Directions, 1968.

―――. *Selected Letters*. Edited by R. D. Paige. New York: New Directions, 1968.

Proust, Marcel. *Swann's Way*. Translated by C. K. Scott Moncrieff and Terence Kilmartin. Franklin Center, Pa.: Franklin Library, 1983.

Pym, Barbara. *A Glass of Blessings*. Harmondsworth, Middlesex, England: Penguin Books, 1980.

Ritzer, George. *Sociological Theory*. New York: Knopf, 1983.

Rossen, Janice. *The World of Barbara Pym*. London: Macmillan Press Ltd., 1987.

Russell, Bertrand. "Logical Atomism." In *Logical Positivism*, edited by A. J. Ayer. New York: Free Press, 1959.

Ryle, Gilbert. "The Thinking of Thoughts." In *Collected Papers*. Vol. 2. London: Hutchinson & Co., 1971.

Said, Edward. *Orientalism*. New York: Pantheon Books, 1978.

Saussure, Ferdinand de. *Course in General Linguistics*. Translated by Wade Baskin. Suffolk: Fontana/Collins, 1974.

Skinner, John. *The Fictions of Anita Brookner*. London: Macmillan, 1992.

Spearman, Charles Edward. *Abilities of Man: Their Nature and Measurement*. London: Macmillan and Co., Limited, 1927.

Sternberg, Robert J. *Beyond I. Q.: A Triarchic Theory of Human Intelligence*. New York: Cambridge University Press, 1985.

Strawson, P. F. *The Bounds of Sense*. London: Methuen, 1966.

―――. *Introduction to Logical Theory*. London: Methuen and Company, 1952.

Thurstone, Louis Leon. *Factorial Studies of Intelligence*. Chicago: University of Chicago Press, 1941.

Toulmin, Stephen. "The Concept of 'Stages' in Psychological Development." In *Cognitive Development and Epistemology*, edited by Theodore Mischel. New York: Academic Press, 1971.

―――. *Cosmopolis: The Hidden Agenda of Modernity*. Chicago: University of Chicago Press, 1992.

―――. *Human Understanding*, Vol. 1: *The Collective Use and Evolution of Concepts*. Princeton: Princeton University Press, 1972.

―――. *The Uses of Argument*. London: Cambridge University Press, 1964.

Trilling, Lionel. "Why We Read Jane Austen." In *The Times Literary Supplement*, no. 3860, March 5, 1976.

Turner, Jonathan H. *The Structure of Sociological Theory*, 4th ed. Belmont, Calif.: Wadsworth Publishing Company, 1986.

Vernon, Philip Ewart. *The Measurement of Abilities*. London: University of London Press, 1940.

Wittgenstein, Ludwig. *Philosophical Investigations*, 3rd ed. Translated by G.E.M. Anscombe. New York: Macmillan, 1968.

———. *Tractatus Logico-Philosophicus*. Translated by C. K. Ogden and F. P. Ramsey. London: Kegan Paul, Trench, Trubner & Co., 1922.

———. *Tractatus Logico-Philosophicus*. Translated by D. F. Pears and B. F. McGuinness. London: Routledge & Kegan Paul, 1961.

Index

About the Author

MARTIN SCHIRALLI is Associate Professor, Faculty of Education, Queen's University, Ontario, Canada.

ISBN 0-89789-695-5

90000>

EAN

9 780897 896955

HARDCOVER BAR CODE